Let's Grow!

Foundations for discipling children

Daphne Kirk

First published in 2001 by
KEVIN MAYHEW LTD
Buxhall
Stowmarket
Suffolk IP14 3BW

9 8 7 6 5 4 3 2 1 0

ISBN 1 84003 740 7
Catalogue No 1500431

Designed by Angela Palfrey
Edited by Helen Elliot

Printed and bound in Great Britain

Contents

Psalm 78:4 and 6
'. . . we will tell the next generation the praiseworthy deeds
of the Lord, his power, and the wonders he has done . . .
so that the next generation would know them, even the children
yet to be born, and they in turn would tell their children.'

Introduction

Let's Grow! is a tool for discipleship. It can be used in a variety of settings but perhaps the most effective will be in the context of child and parent.

The adult is named a 'special friend' in the material so this can be applied to a parent or responsible adult.

The following guidelines will help you to achieve the best from the time spent with your child. Meet with one child at a time; each child is different!

1. Anticipate that you will change and grow with the child; apply the material to yourself also.

2. Try to have one session a week with your child (values cannot be changed every day!).

3. *Let's Grow!* aims to stimulate sharing and deepen relationships, so take your time together in a relaxed, quiet environment.

4. The material is not designed to answer questions, but to reveal issues that need to be talked through.

5. If you are not the parent, always gain the permission of the parent. Show them the material. Ask if they would like to join you as you meet with the child. Stay in a place where you can be seen and heard by others, i.e. not behind closed doors.

6. Remember that honest answers are 'right' answers.

7. If you are unsure how to react, or unsure of an answer, it is all right to tell the child that you will talk about it again the next time you meet, and take some time to pray or ask for help.

8. Find creative ways to learn the memory verse, i.e. put actions to it, draw a picture of it, miss out words, make them into plaques, etc.

Remember that this is one of the most important times with your child. You have all the wisdom and anointing of the Holy Spirit available to you. Enjoy your time . . . have fun and expect Jesus to be at the centre!

My name is: _____

My friend is: _____

My church is: _____

_____

_____

We will meet on: _____

_____

My address is: _____

_____

_____

_____

_____

Certificate

has completed these units with

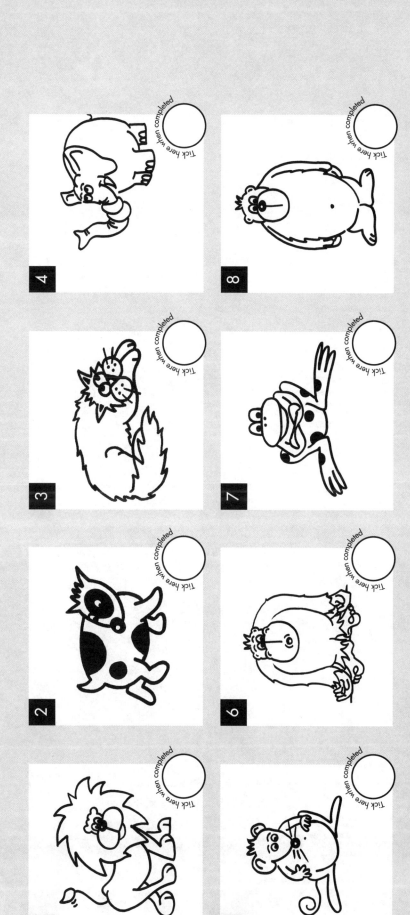

1 Tick here when completed

2 Tick here when completed

3 Tick here when completed

4 Tick here when completed

5 Tick here when completed

6 Tick here when completed

7 Tick here when completed

8 Tick here when completed

Unit 1
Welcome to God's family

11

Welcome to God's family

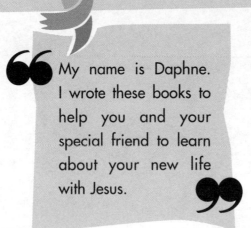

" My name is Daphne. I wrote these books to help you and your special friend to learn about your new life with Jesus. "

Welcome to God's family

I wonder why you decided to follow Jesus?

Perhaps you could tell me why.

I decided to follow Jesus because _____

_____

_____

_____

_____

_____

Before you accepted Jesus you did many things without even thinking about what He wanted. Now it is difficult to think what your new life will be like.

Some toys come with an instruction book – and if we want to use the toy properly we need to read the book, otherwise we might play with it and not know all the wonderful things it can do.

It would be sad if we did not know all the wonderful things about our new life with Jesus. The Bible is our instruct book – **and we'll learn how to use it together.**

Tell me some things you think will make you happy, or happier.

I'd be happy if..

....

I'd be happy if..

....

I'd be happy if..

....

I'd be happy if..

....

Here are some things you might think will make you happy . . .

School

A holiday

New clothes

New friends

A new toy

Q **These things will bring you happiness, but is it happiness that will last?**

Yes/No

The answer is 'No' because things change – better toys come into the shops – holidays come to an end – friends are not always kind to us – clothes become too small – and then our happiness goes too.

Your new life with Jesus is different. You have given your life to Jesus to take care of. He thinks you are more precious and valuable than anything you can imagine.

What is the most precious thing you can think of?

_____

_____

_____

You are so precious to Jesus that He died for you,
so you can trust Him to take care of your life.

Read Matthew 6:26

What does your Father God feed?

_____

Now either draw, or find a picture to stick in this book of someone
who is more valuable than the birds are . . .

Memory Verse

● This is your verse to learn this week. You can learn it and then say it to your special friend, or perhaps you could learn it together!

For God so loved the world
that He gave His one and only Son,
that whoever believes in Him
shall not perish but have eternal life.

John 3:16

More sharing together

1. Talk together about someone who is very precious to both of you.

2. Then both of you write your own letter to them telling them why you love them.

   Take the letters to them together this week.

To my special friend

Where do you belong?

Where do you belong?

Read Luke 1:31-33

Q How long will the Kingdom last?
A day or 1000 years or for ever?

Q Who is the king of the Kingdom of God?
Is it King Arthur or Jesus or Henry VIII?

" I have something to tell you that sounds like a riddle – but it is true. Sometimes we can't understand everything about the Kingdom of God but we can just be excited and believe it. Are you ready? I'm going to tell you something wonderful. "

You are IN God's Kingdom
AND
God's Kingdom is IN you because
Jesus is in you.

see Luke 17:21

WOW!

Complete this certificate about your birthday

Birth Certificate

Name: ....

Mother's name: ....

Father's name: ....

Date of birth: ....

Place of birth: ....

Citizen of: ....

You now have another birthday – when you were 'born again' into God's Kingdom.

Born Again Certificate

Name: ....

Date of your new birthday: ....

Place where you were born again: ....

Citizen of the .... of God.

You are now able to hear Jesus speaking to you!

You are a very special person. Why do you think you are very special?

I think I am special because _____

_____

_____

You are not special because of anything you have done.
You are special just because you are . . .

_____

(put your name here)

Isn't that exciting news?

_____

We are going to discover many exciting
things together – and as you introduce your
friends to **King Jesus** they will
belong to the Kingdom of God too.

Memory Verse

● This is your verse to learn this week. You can learn it and then say it to your special friend, or perhaps you could learn it together!

He will reign . . .
for ever and ever;
His Kingdom will
never end.

Luke 1:33

More sharing together

1. Share together what happened when you took the letters last week.

2. Ask your special friend to tell you about when they were born again into God's Kingdom, then ask them questions about it.

This week, go together to one other person and ask them how they were born again.

Who are your family?

Who are your family?

God's plan is that all babies have a family –
a mother, a father, relatives or someone who loves and cares for them.

Have you got a photo of those special people?
If not, you could draw them.

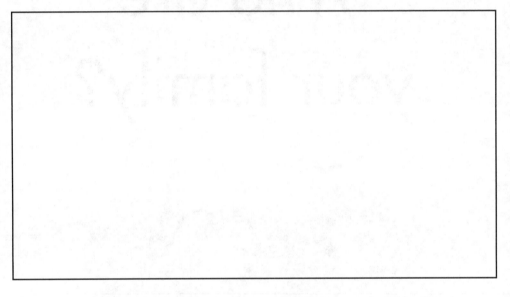

When you became a Christian you became part of a new family.

Read Ephesians 2:19

We are now members of the family of

_____

The first Christians went to each other's homes,
ate meals together and had fun together, just like a family!

What do you think **'church'** is?

_____

It is all the people in God's **family**.

Jesus also calls it His **body**.

26

The church is made up of different people.

Tell me about your **church**.

Your **church group leader** is _____

Some other members of my church are: _____

_____

_____

_____

_____

As people come to know Jesus, God's family grows bigger and bigger.

A family gets bigger when a new child is born.

God's family gets bigger when someone is **BORN AGAIN!**

I think that is very exciting, don't you?

Memory Verse

● This is your verse to learn this week. You can learn it and then say it to your special friend, or perhaps you could learn it together!

I am the way and the truth
and the life.
No one comes to the Father
except through Me.

John 14:6

More sharing together

1. Can you remember what happened when you asked the other person how they were born again? Talk about it together.

Ask your special friend to tell you about their family or about other church families they have been in.

Caring in the family

Caring in the family

Q **Have you just become a Christian?** _____ You will have **TWO** birthdays and **TWO** ages.

You were born to your parents on .... and you are .... years old.
(Your physical birthday.)

**You were born into the family of God on ....
and you are now .... years old.**
(Your spiritual birthday.)

You need to grow physically, so you look after your body eating, exercising, washing, and keeping it warm.

Q When you were 1 week old what did you eat?

_____

When you were 1 year old what did you eat?

_____

What do you eat today?

_____

Who looked after you as a baby and made sure you had the right food?

_____

You now need to grow and learn in the Kingdom of God.

Hebrews 5:12 says that when we begin our life in the Kingdom of God we are babies who can drink only _ _ _ _ and are not old enough for solid _ _ _ _.

The 'milk' here means teaching from the Bible that you need when you first become a Christian. You will need others to 'feed' you the right food at the right time from the Bible.

I will help you as we journey together.

Your friend ....
who is meeting with you each week will help you too.

Who are the other people who can help you eat the right food in the Kingdom of God and help you to learn what is good and evil?

_____

_____

_____

_____

Memory Verse

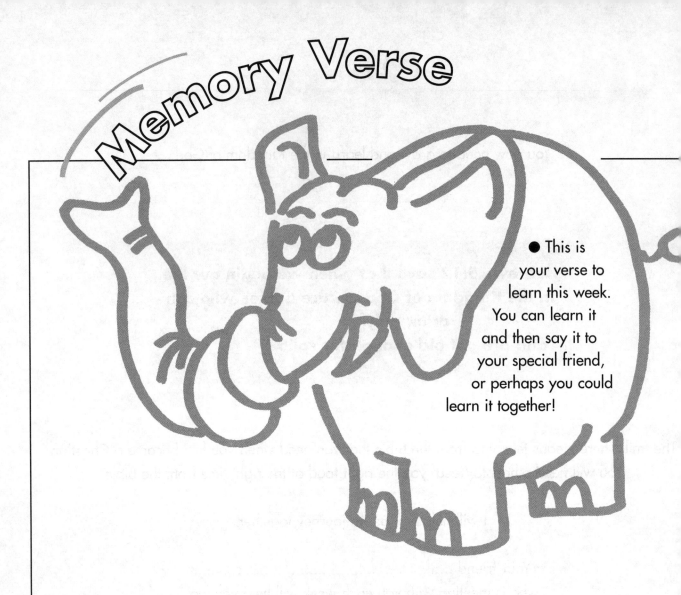

● This is your verse to learn this week. You can learn it and then say it to your special friend, or perhaps you could learn it together!

Peace I leave with you;

my peace I give you . . .

Do not let your hearts

be troubled and do not

be afraid.

John 14:27

More sharing together

1. Talk together about the Bible.

2. Did your special friend find the Bible easy to understand when they were a child?

3. Who helped your friend to understand the Bible?

4. What do you find difficult about the Bible?

5. How can your friend help you?

Your new body

Your new body

I'd like you to draw a picture or put a photo of yourself here.

You are a very special and important person

Can you say to your eye that you don't need it?	Yes/No
Can you say to your hand that you don't need it?	Yes/No
Can you say to your feet that you don't need them?	Yes/No

We need all of our body – each part is important and special. It is very sad when there is something wrong with one part of it.

Can you say to the people of your church that you don't need them?

NO! Remember that every part of the body is needed and important, just like your eye, hand and feet.

Each part of your body cares for the other parts.

Draw lines to show what one part does for the other parts. I've done one for you!

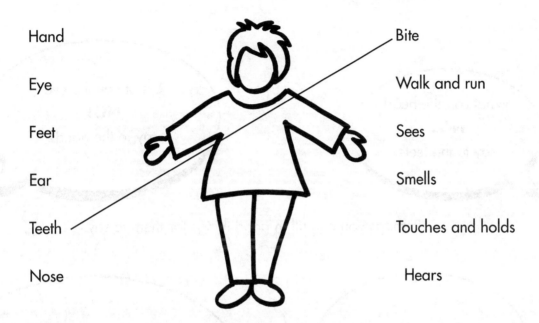

Hand   Bite

Eye   Walk and run

Feet   Sees

Ear   Smells

Teeth   Touches and holds

Nose   Hears

It is important that in Jesus' body each part cares
for the rest and does what it can to help them.

What could you do to show another member of your church
that you really care about them?

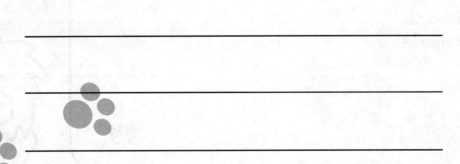

Remember, there will be times when you don't like something another person in your church does.

You may not like what they **DO** but that is never a reason not to like **THEM**.

Now read 1 Corinthians 12:18-21
(If you find reading easy then you might like to read from verse 14 to 21 and you will be able to understand most of it now.)

What can the head
NOT
say to the feet?

What can the eye
NOT
say to the hand?

Perhaps you can fill in good things for them to say.

What could you say to other members of your church?

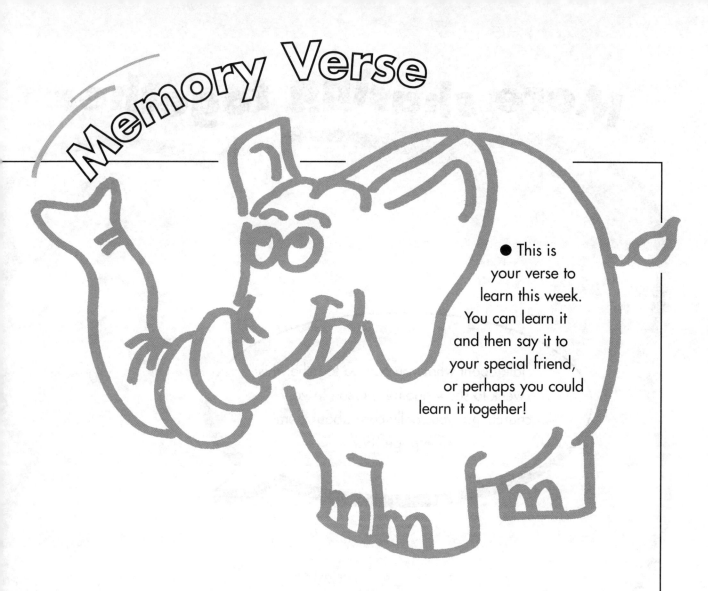

Memory Verse

● This is your verse to learn this week. You can learn it and then say it to your special friend, or perhaps you could learn it together!

God has arranged
the parts in the body,
every one of them,
just as He wanted
them to be.

1 Corinthians 12:18

More sharing together

1. Talk about what you can do together this week to show another person in your church that you really care about them. (See page 39.)

2. Plan when you will do it.

3. Pray together about it.

Growing up in your family

Growing up in your family

As you grew up in your family you learnt about things being

right (good)

and **wrong** (bad)

Give a tick or a cross to show which of these you
have learned to be right or wrong.

Playing around with knives. ☐

Cleaning your teeth. ☐

Running across the road. ☐

Telling the truth. ☐

Tidying up your bedroom. ☐

Hurting people. ☐

Sharing your toys. ☐

Bullying other children. ☐

In the family of God we continue to learn about things that are right, and
things that are wrong.

If we do things that are wrong, someone usually gets hurt.
So it is good for everyone if we try to do things that are right.

If you are **playing around with knives**, who might get hurt? _____

If you are **bullying other children**, who might get hurt? _____

So there may be things that you will have to fight. Circle any of these that give you trouble:

Hating   Fear   Disobedience

Not forgiving

Lying   Being too proud

God has given us a sword to fight Satan with.

Read Ephesians 6:17

The sword of the Spirit which is the _ _ _ _ **of G** _ _ **(or the B** _ _ _ _ **).**

That's good news, isn't it?
The more we grow as Christians –
and the more we know the Bible – the better we will be
able to fight Satan
and **WIN**.

_____
(Put your name here.)

**is
a winner
with
Jesus**

45

When you find something difficult, who do you ask to help you?

_____

When you find it hard to fight against some of the things that are wrong . . .

remember . . .

you are in God's family and He is your Father.
We have **prayer** which is like a telephone line to Him. You can ask Him to help you.

You are a member of God's family.
Tick the box that tells you when you can talk to your heavenly Father:

Only in my church ☐

Only on Sunday ☐

Only with my friend ☐

Only when I am in trouble ☐

At any time and anywhere ☐

The last box was the right answer.

You can talk to God any time and anywhere.

Memory Verse

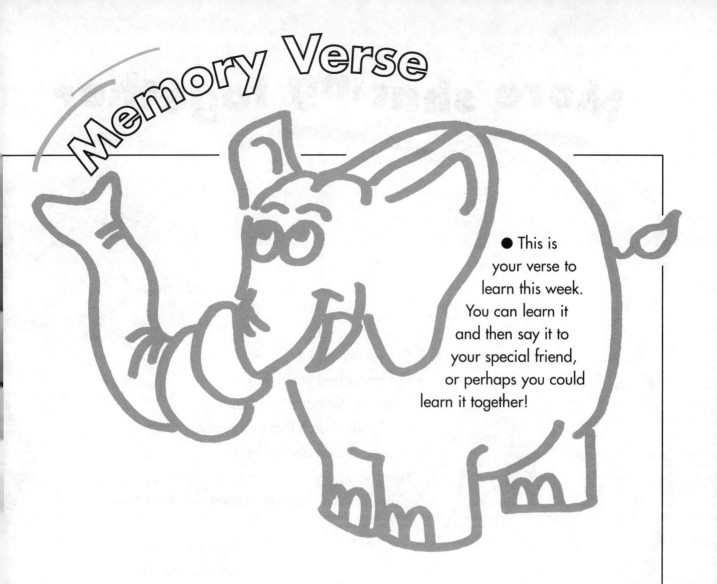

● This is your verse to learn this week. You can learn it and then say it to your special friend, or perhaps you could learn it together!

Take the
helmet of salvation
and the sword of the Spirit,
which is the
Word of God.

Ephesians 6:17

More sharing together

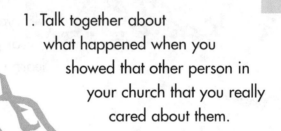

1. Talk together about
what happened when you
showed that other person in
your church that you really
cared about them.

2. Pray together for them now.

3. Ask your special
friend what they have
trouble with
(see page 45) and
ask how they fight it.

4 Pray for your
special friend.

Both of you, please write your favourite verse from this unit here

If you have any questions from this unit,
write them here to ask your special friend.

_____

_____

_____

_____

_____

_____

_____

_____

_____

_____

51

Unit 2
Special times and gifts

Baptism

Baptism

There are some very special times you will share with your church.

Read Mark 1:9-11

What did John do for Jesus?

He b _ _ _ _ _ _ _ Him.

Baptism is when someone who is following Jesus goes into the water, right under it and then comes up again.

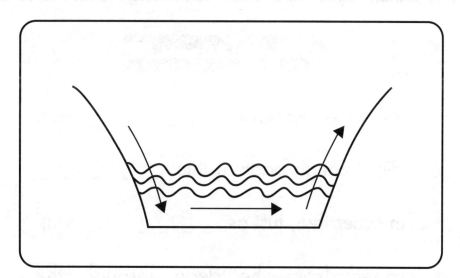

Jesus died on the cross, was buried in the grave and came alive again.

So we show that our old life is dead and buried and that we have a new life in the Kingdom of Go

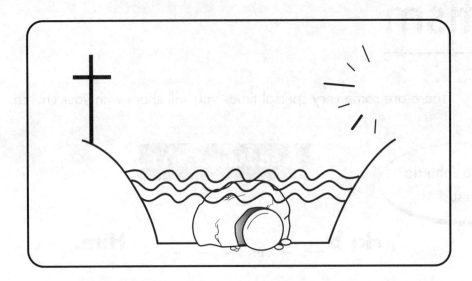

**Being baptised is really important.
It is something Jesus did and something He told us to do.**

Now read Romans 6:4

We were therefore _ _ _ _ _ _ with

Him through baptism into _ _ _ _ _

in order that, just as _ _ _ _ _ _ was

raised from the dead through the

glory of the _ _ _ _ _ _ , we too may

live a _ _ _ _ _ _ _ .

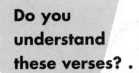

**Do you
understand
these verses? . . .** If you said 'No', your
special friend will help you.

Can you draw the special pictures
that tell us all about being baptised?

Baptism is when someone who is following
Jesus goes into the water, right under it and then comes up again.

Jesus died on the cross, was buried in the grave and came alive again.

So we show that our old life is dead and buried and we have a new life in the Kingdom of God.

Being baptised is really important.
It is something Jesus did and something He told us to do.

Q Where in the Bible is this explained to us?

Have you ever seen anyone baptised?   Yes / No

If you have, could you tell me about it, or
draw a picture?

Memory Verse

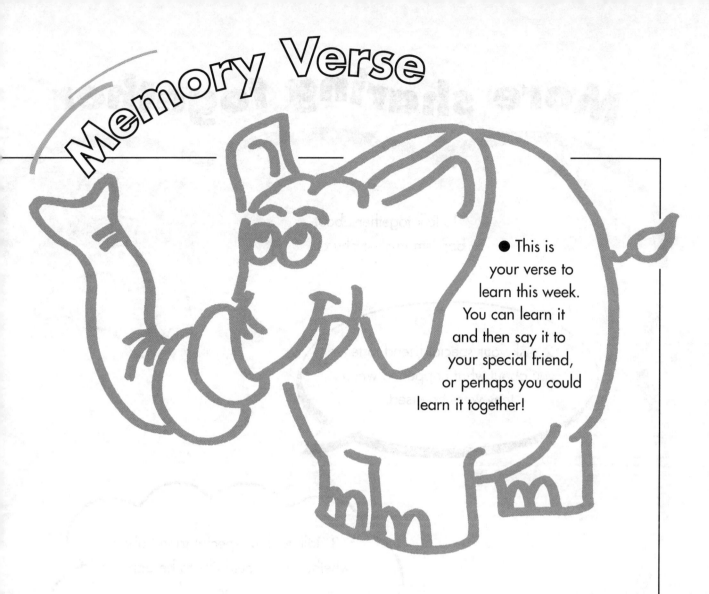

● This is your verse to learn this week. You can learn it and then say it to your special friend, or perhaps you could learn it together!

Just as Jesus was raised from the dead
through the glory of the Father,
so we too may live
a new life.

Romans 6:4

More sharing together

1. Talk together about baptism in your church.

2. Ask your special friend to tell you about what happened when they were baptised.

3. Talk to your special friend about whether you would like to be baptised
or,
if you have been baptised, tell your friend what happened.

Baptism . . . baptism . . . baptism . . .

4. At church this week, with your friend, find someone who has been baptised and ask them about their baptism.

The Lord's Supper

The Lord's Supper

Q **Have you taken part in a special meal called the 'Lord's Supper'?**

It is another very special time that you will share with your church family.

Here is a letter to you from Jesus:

Dear _____ (put your name here)

I'd like you to share my meal! Your birthday is a special time when people remember you. This meal is a special time to remember me. The night before I died for you, I had a meal with my special friends. I told them to remember my death by sharing that meal. Every time they ate it they remembered that I died for them.

Now that you are a part of my family I want you to remember that I died especially for you. Eat this meal and share it with your church family. I will be there too.

You did not do anything to make me love you this much. I just loved you.

As you eat, remember that because I died, your old life is dead too.

I love you. I loved you yesterday and I will love you tomorrow; nothing you do can change my love for you.

I love you very much.
Jesus

That was a special letter, wasn't it?
It was from Jesus to you.

Write a letter from you to Jesus; perhaps you would like to read it to your special friend.
If you find writing hard, a special picture for Him would be wonderful.

Jesus will see what you write to Him and it will make Him very pleased that you wrote back.

Date ——————

Dear Jesus,

Now I would like your specia
friend to read you the letter
from Jesus.
Then you read the letter you
have written to Jesus.

Read Matthew 26:26-36

This is the special meal that Jesus had with His disciples before He died.
It is the meal He asks us to remember Him by.

n you draw a picture
what is happening in
rse 26?

d now can you draw
at is happening in
ses 27 and 28?

Have you taken part in the Lord's Supper?

_____

What do you think about being able to take part in it?

Memory Verse

● This is your verse to learn this week. You can learn it and then say it to your special friend, or perhaps you could learn it together!

The Lord Jesus . . .
took bread . . . broke it
and said,
'This is my body
which is given for you.
Do this in remembrance of me.'

1 Corinthians 11:23, 24

More sharing together

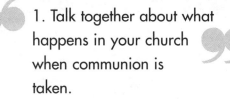 1. Talk together about what happens in your church when communion is taken.

2. **Do you all take the Lord's Supper?**

3. **Ask your special friend to talk to you about what your church says about children taking communion.**

4. **What do you both feel when you take the Lord's Supper?**

5. Now get some bread and juice and share the Lord's Supper together IF your special friend thinks this would be right.

Being filled with the Spirit

Being filled with the Spirit

When you received Jesus you were given His Holy Spirit.
He lives in you all the time. We make the Holy Spirit unhappy when we do naughty things.
Fill this fruit in with some of the things that make Him unhappy.

There is a fruit that the Holy Spirit can give.

Read Galatians 5:22

and fill in all the good things in the Holy Spirit's fruit.

L _____
F _____
J _____
K _____
P _____
S _____
P _____
G _____
G _____

Which of these good things do you think you would like to be seen in your life? Choose two that you especially need because you find them hard.

Which of these good things did Jesus have?

We need **HELP** to grow that fruit in our lives!

Jesus knows we need help, so if we ask, He says
He will fill us up with the POWER of the Holy Spirit.

Answer this question very carefully. It is very important . . .

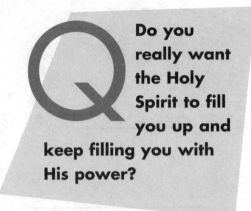

Q Do you really want the Holy Spirit to fill you up and keep filling you with His power?

Read Ephesians 5:18b

and cross out the wrong words below . . .

Be empty/half full/filled with the Spirit.

Jesus said He would fill us with the Spirit if we asked.

Does Jesus always do what He says He will do?

Would you like to ask the Holy Spirit to fill you up?

If you have said 'yes' in both the boxes your special friend will pray for you and

you will be filled with
the Holy Spirit

Memory Verse

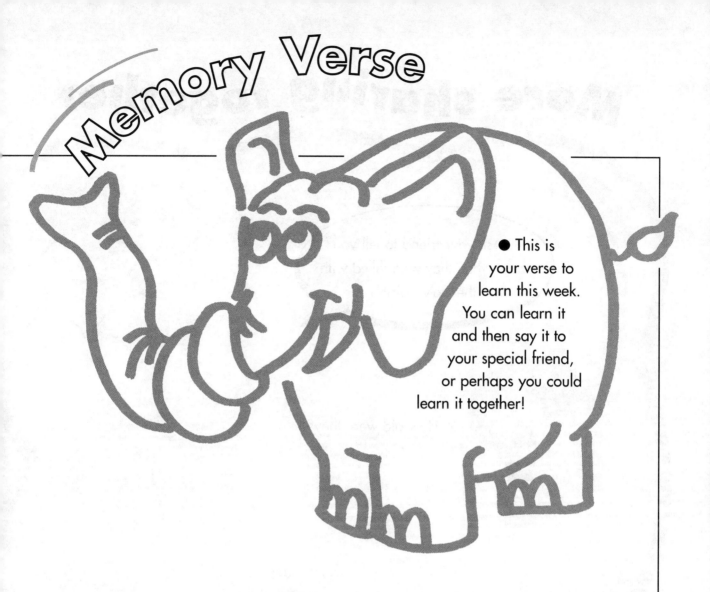

● This is your verse to learn this week. You can learn it and then say it to your special friend, or perhaps you could learn it together!

The fruit of the Spirit is love,
joy, peace, patience,
kindness, goodness, faithfulness,
gentleness and self-control.

Galatians 5:22

More sharing together

1. Ask your friend to tell you about when they were filled with the Holy Spirit.

2. How old were they?

5. Are they glad that the Holy Spirit filled them?

3. Who was with them?

4. What happened afterwards?

6. Now tell them what you feel about being filled with the Holy Spirit.

More gifts

More gifts

Who does the Holy Spirit want to give gifts to?

E _ e _ y _ n _

I want to tell you about two more of these gifts.

Q

Have you heard anyone 'speaking in tongues'?

It is a very special language given as a gift by the Holy Spirit.
You may already speak in your own special language.

When someone speaks in tongues in your church group or celebration,
the Holy Spirit will tell someone else to say what it means
so that it helps people who are listening to understand.

Like this . . .

Holy Spirit

| Your special language | The meaning of the special language |

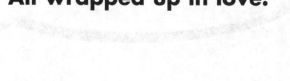

All wrapped up in love.

Your special language is a prayer language.

Read 1 Corinthians 14:2

'Anyone who speaks in a tongue

does not speak to _ _ _ but

to _ _ _ .'

This is
wonderful!

Sometimes we don't know what to pray, then the
Holy Spirit will pray for us in the special prayer language and Jesus will understand.

Have you spoken in this very special language? _____

Have you been filled up with the Holy Spirit? _____

If you said 'No' to the first question and 'Yes'
to the second question,
then your special friend will talk to you about it.

80

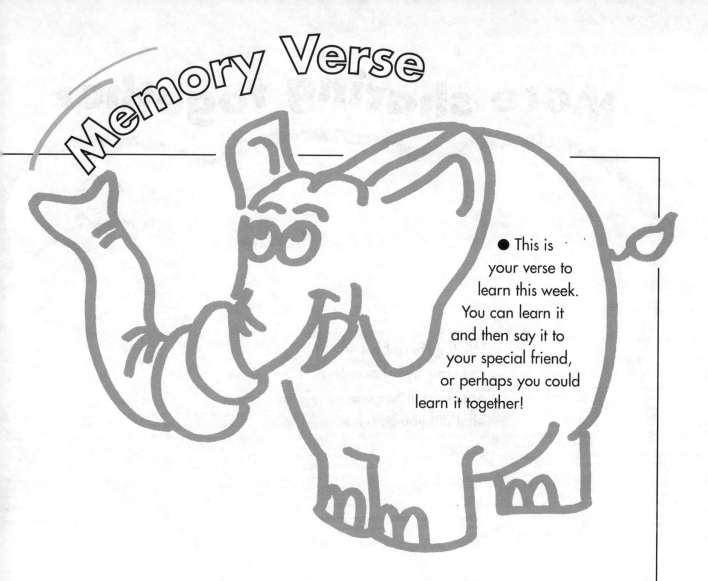

Memory Verse

● This is your verse to learn this week. You can learn it and then say it to your special friend, or perhaps you could learn it together!

If I speak in the tongues
of men and of angels,
but have not love,
I am only
a clanging cymbal.

1 Corinthians 13:1

More sharing together

1. Talk together about where you have heard people speaking in tongues – what did you both feel?

My special language

This means ....

2. Share about times when you both heard someone speaking in tongues and another person speaking out what they felt it meant in English.

The Spirit's power

The Spirit's power

Q **Do you like receiving presents or gifts?**

What is the best gift you have ever had?

Have you ever received a gift that was for giving away?

Have you noticed that the Kingdom of God is different from the kingdom of the world?

**Here is a big difference –
when we are filled with the Holy Spirit**

He gives us gifts for giving away

Holy Spirit   I give you power      so you can serve.

The Spirit's power

Holy Spirit   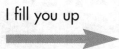I fill you up      so that the fruit

will make others happy.

Holy Spirit   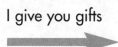I give you gifts      to give to others.

85

As you enjoy Jesus and spend time with Him you will find that there are some very special ways that He will use you.

I will be happy!

Gifts given to me to give away.

What has Jesus given you that you can give away?

He has given me

_____

to give away.

Memory Verse

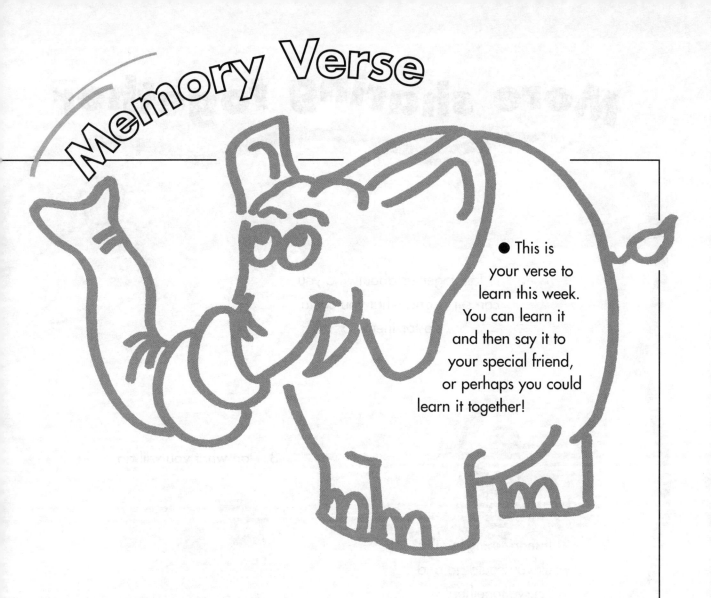

● This is your verse to learn this week. You can learn it and then say it to your special friend, or perhaps you could learn it together!

Follow the way of love, and eagerly desire spiritual gifts.

1 Corinthians 14:1

More sharing together

" 1. Talk together about who you can serve and what you could do for them. "

2. Is there someone this week you could go and serve together?

3. Plan what you will do.

4. Will this make them happier?

5. Pray together about what you plan to do.

If you have any questions from this unit, write them here to ask your special friend.

_____

_____

_____

_____

_____

_____

_____

_____

Unit 3
Talking and listening

Talking and
listening

Talking and listening

> Have you ever noticed that when you spend time with a friend two things happen, talking and listening. It is no fun talking to someone if they don't listen to what you say!

I talk

I listen

THEN

I talk

I listen

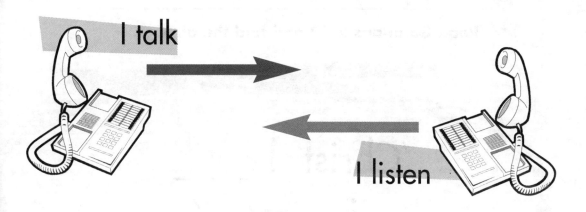

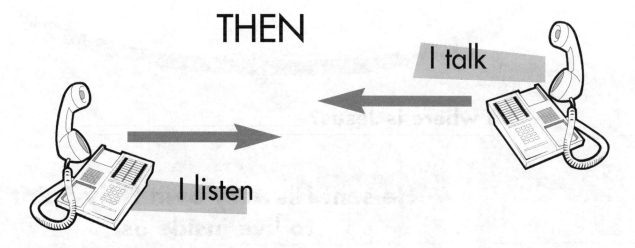

Have you ever thought that when we spend time with God the same needs to happen:

talking and listening.

7

> It is hard to listen to someone if you don't know where they are, so if you are going to listen to God you need to know where He is.

Where do you think He is? _____

Read Galatians 2:20 and find the answer.

'Christ I _ _ _ _
i _ m _ .'

So where is Jesus? _____

He sent His very own Holy Spirit to live inside us.

Have you ever heard Jesus speaking to you? _____
If you said 'Yes', tell me about it.

_____

_____

_____

There is a lovely story in
1 Samuel 3:2-11.
I'd like you to read it together right now.

Q **Have you read the story?** Yes/No

Was Samuel a child? _____
Did he hear God very clearly? _____
**Do you think that you could hear Him
      speaking to you?** _____

**I think this story is so special I'd like
      you to draw a picture of it.**

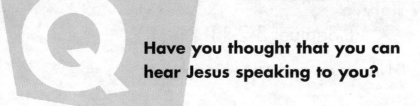

Have you thought that you can hear Jesus speaking to you?

Remember that HE is in YOU!

I want you to LISTEN now.

You will hear Him deep inside you (that is, in your spirit).

Just say

 Speak to me, Jesus. I am listening.

Then close your eyes and be very quiet.

After a few moments open your eyes and write in the box what you feel He says to you.

Jesus says to me
'I think you are_____'

then put any other things you think He is saying to you:
'

_____

_____ '

_____

Memory Verse

● This is your verse to learn this week. You can learn it and then say it to your special friend, or perhaps you could learn it together!

Christ lives in me . . .
I live by faith
in the Son of God.

Galatians 2:20

More sharing together

Sometimes Jesus gives us pictures.

They may mean something to you
or they may mean something
to another person.

I'd like you both to ask Jesus for a picture, just like you
asked to hear His voice. If you do not understand the
picture He gives you, don't worry, your special friend
will talk to you about it. You may be able to talk to
your special friend about the picture they get, too.

Close your eyes and ask Jesus to give you a picture that will help you to know Him better.

Then open your eyes and draw the picture He has given you.

My picture from Jesus

My special friend's picture from Jesus

Who is important?

 # Who is important?

Jesus spent time TALKING to His Father and LISTENING to His Father.

Read Luke 5:16

Where did Jesus go to pray?   L _ _ _ _ _   P _ _ _ _ _ .

He went where He could be quiet to hear His Father deep inside Him (in His Spirit).

How many times did He do it?   O _ _ _ _

Now read Luke 6:12.

Where did He go this time to pray?   The m _ _ _ _ _ _ _ _ _ _ _ .

Do you think that Jesus thought it was important to spend time talking and listening to His Father?   Yes/No

I think Jesus thought it was very important.

There are some things that we think are important, like playing with friends or watching television. Make a list of things that are important to YOU.

_____   _____

_____   _____

_____   _____

_____

I wonder if you have put prayer on your list?

Do you think Jesus would have put PRAYER on His list?

_____

You have special friends who you like spending time with.

Who are these friends?

_____

_____

_____

_____

Jesus is a very special friend.

Is He on your list?

He loves to spend time talking with you. He has a list of special friends.

Do you think you are on His list?

YES ✔

You are on Jesus' list. He loves the times you spend
talking and **listening** together.

Do you remember **talking** and **listening** with God
in the previous session of this unit? _____

I want you both to listen to Him again today.
You will hear Him deep inside you (in your spirit).

If you close your eyes it will help you to listen more carefully.

Say 'Speak to me, Jesus. I am listening.
What do you want to say to me about your love?'

Then open your eyes and write down what He says to you.

<table>
<tr><td>

Jesus says to me

'My love is _____

_____

_____'

and then write anything else you
think He is saying to you.

_____

_____

_____

</td><td>

Jesus says to my friend

'My love is _____

_____

_____'

and then write anything else you
think He is saying.

_____

_____

_____

</td></tr>
</table>

Memory Verse

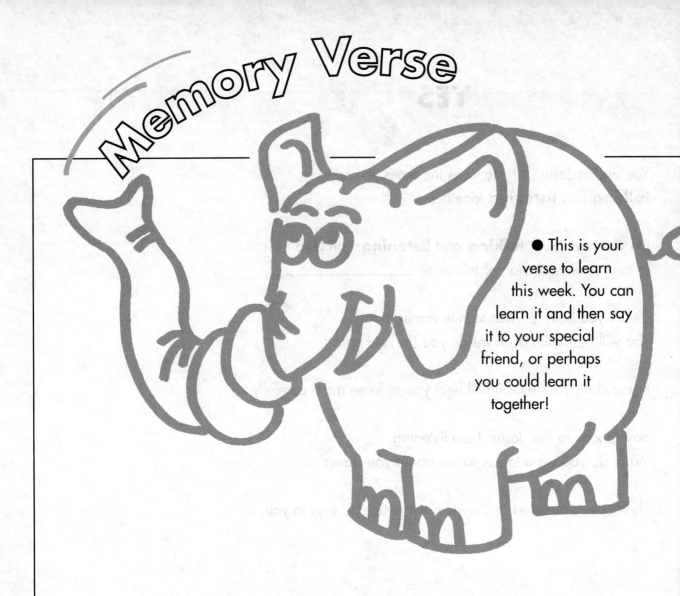

● This is your verse to learn this week. You can learn it and then say it to your special friend, or perhaps you could learn it together!

I pray for those
who will believe in Me . . .
that all of them
may be one.

John 17:20-21

More sharing together

Ask Jesus to speak to you both about something you have done this session. He may give you and your special friend some words, or a picture. If He gives you a picture, write underneath what you think He is saying to you in it. Your special friend will help you with your message if you need it, but have a go at doing it by yourself first if you can. Remember to sit quietly with Jesus.

Choose one thing you would like Him to talk to you about and say

Lord Jesus, please talk to me about . . .

You

Lord Jesus, please talk to me about . . .

Your special friend

Checking
it out!

Checking it out!

How do you think the men who wrote the Bible knew what to write?

_____

The answer is that Jesus' Holy Spirit told them what to put. You have the Holy Spirit in you.

He will also speak to you.

He will always agree with the Bible.

It is really important that we know and understand, deep inside (in our spirit), what the Holy Spirit is saying to us in the Bible.

This is what happens –

> **We read with our eyes.**
>
> **What we read goes into our mind.**
>
> **It can drop into our heart like this**

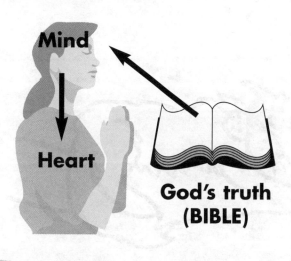

Mind

Heart

**God's truth
(BIBLE)**

113

There are parts of the Bible that are hard to understand.
That is why I am helping you – and why
you have your special friend.

It is important that you share what Jesus says to
you with your special friend, until you know the
Bible well enough to check that what you have
written agrees with the Bible.

Does . . .

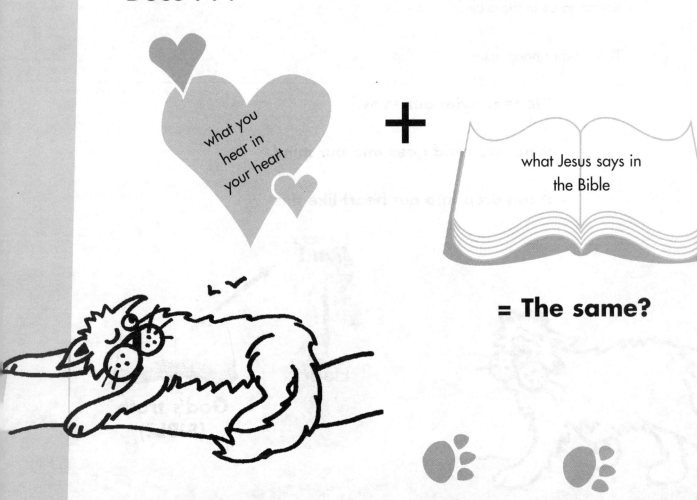

what you
hear in
your heart

+

what Jesus says in
the Bible

= The same?

Tick if the sentences agree with the Bible.
Cross if they are not the same as the Bible.

Jesus loves me very much. ☐

Jesus enjoys the time I spend with Him. ☐

Jesus says, 'Don't eat bananas.' ☐

It is all right to be naughty sometimes. ☐

Jesus says, 'I will never, ever leave you.' ☐

What do a lamp and a light do for us?

Read Psalm 119:105

'Your Word is a _ _ _ _ to my _ _ _ _

and a _ _ _ _ _ for my _ _ _ _ '

So God's Word in the Bible will help us to see clearly the way to go. That is why it is so important that we get to know His Word and check that everything agrees with it.

I am going to share something very special.

Daniella is my little girl and she spends time quietly with Jesus. She reads the Bible and has used *Living with Jesus* to help her. She asked Jesus, 'What do you want to say to me?' Jesus answered her and said:

'I love you and you are precious. Everything you do which I don't like you can cast onto me and I will free you from it. Do what I want you to do, don't let anyone get in your way. You are my daughter and so I treasure you more than anything worth the whole money in the world.'

Does what Daniella wrote agree with the Bible?   Yes/No   The answer is . . . Yes.

Daniella has a special book where she writes down what she hears Jesus saying. She shows her special friend. They enjoy those special words from Jesus to her together.

116

Memory Verse

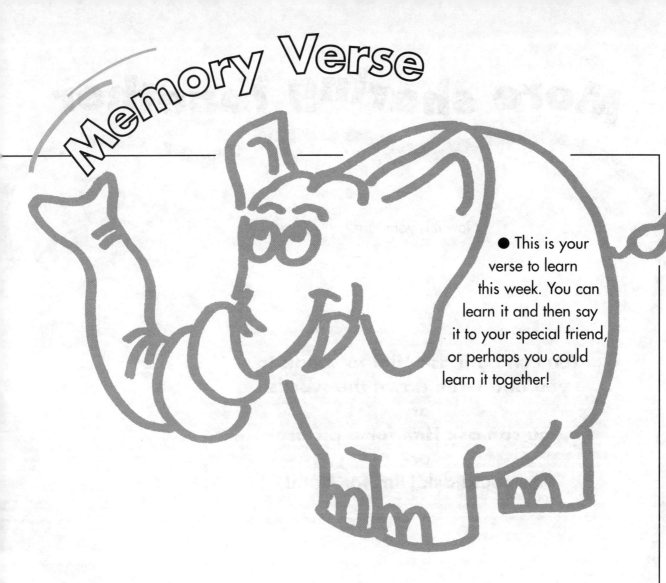

● This is your verse to learn this week. You can learn it and then say it to your special friend, or perhaps you could learn it together!

Your Word is a lamp
to my feet
and a light for my path.

Psalm 119:105

More sharing together

Now it is your turn.

> **You can both ask Him to speak to you and write down the words**
> **or**
> **you can ask Him for a picture**
> **or**
> **you could ask Him for both!**

Your special friend	You

Knowing
His voice

Knowing His voice

Last session I shared with you a page from Daniella's very special book. Daniella said I could share it with you. She listens to Jesus and writes in her book what He says to her.

Here is another page from her book. She always puts the date at the top.

Jesus, what do you want me to do?

I want you to be good and faithful and trust others. Be what I have made you to be and serve those I want you to serve. Don't try too hard, just do your best because I love you and don't want you to be too over the top and try too hard.

Does this agree with the Bible?   Yes/No

The answer is 'Yes'.

Read John 10:2-4

Who calls the sheep? _____

Do the sheep listen to the shepherd? _____

Do the sheep know the voice of the shepherd? _____

Who is our Shepherd? _____

Who are Jesus' sheep? _____

Who **speaks** to us? _____

Do we **listen** to Him? _____

Do we **know** His voice? _____

You know the voice of people you spend time **listening** to. Whose voice do you know really well? _____

It is the same with Jesus. The more time you spend **listening** to Him the better you will know His voice.

I find that <u>**really**</u> exciting.

I'd like you to spend more time **listening** and getting to know the voice of your Shepherd (Jesus).

I have helped you to start, now make sure you have somewhere quiet to be with Jesus and

listen to Him.

Memory Verse

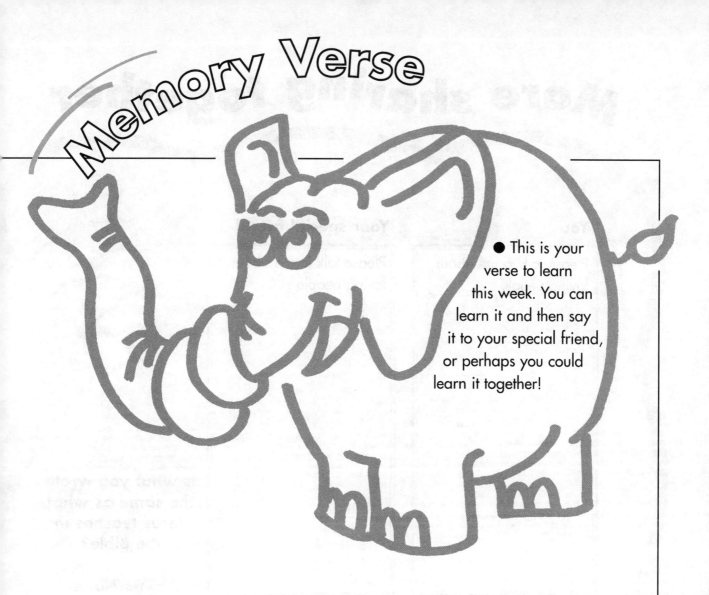

● This is your verse to learn this week. You can learn it and then say it to your special friend, or perhaps you could learn it together!

The sheep listen to His voice.
He calls His own sheep by name
and leads them out.

John 10:3

More sharing together

You

Please talk to me about loving people . . .

Your special friend

Please talk to me about loving people . . .

Is what you wrote the same as what Jesus teaches in the Bible?

Yes/No

I love you very much and I . . .

I love you very much and I . . .

Now read what you have written to each other.

Being with Jesus

Being with Jesus

Read Luke 10:38-42

What were the names of the two ladies who Jesus visited?

_____ and _____

Why was Martha upset in verse 40? _____

_____

One day Jesus arrived at the home of Martha and Mary.

When He arrived Martha rushed around, made the house tidy, cooked special food and tried her best to make sure everything would be perfect for Jesus.

Mary sat and listened to Jesus . . .

Jesus was only visiting. He wouldn't be there long, so who do you think pleased Jesus most?

Mary listened to Jesus so she would know Him a bit better, feel His love a bit more, and hear the things He wanted to tell her.

Jesus loves us to take time out from all the things we are so busy doing and spend time just being with Him – like Mary.

Now answer these questions, but think very carefully about the answers . .

How much does Jesus love you? _____

Does He love you **more** when you are good?_____

Does He love you **less** when you are naughty?_____

Does He love you **more** if you do something very well?_____

Does He love you **less** if you are not very good at something? _____

I am going to share something with you that many people, adults and children, do not understand in their hearts.

Jesus loves to share in the things you **DO**.
He enjoys **DOING** things with you.
He is happy when you **DO** something well.
He is sad when something you DO goes wrong.

BUT

**Jesus loves you with a special kind of love.
It is called *agape* love.
That means His love for you is always the same.
If you never did anything for Him
He would still love you.
When you are naughty His love for
you does not change one little bit.**

He loves *(agape)* you so much no one
can measure His love for YOU.

**Now read this aloud to your special friend,
then let your special friend read it to you.**

He loves me when I'm good.

He loves me when I'm naughty.

He loves me when I'm happy.

He loves me when I'm sad.

He loves me when I'm doing something well.

He loves me when I do something badly.

He loves me just because I am

(Put your name here.)

_____

(Special friend put your name here.)

_____

129

Now I want you to spend a few moments being like Mary – don't be in a hurry, like Martha was!

Sit down and make sure everything is quiet around you.

Have this book and your pencil with you.

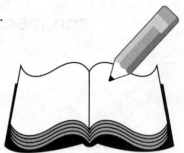

Now close your eyes and imagine that you are sitting at Jesus' feet, like Mary did.

Spend a few moments imagining it with your eyes closed.

Now both of you write down what you think Jesus is saying to you as you sit at His feet.

You may want to stop now, and return to this book another time. Then you could ask Jesus for a picture as you sit at His feet. Or you may want to spend a bit longer with Him now, and ask Him to give you a picture, too.

My picture from Jesus . . .

Memory Verse

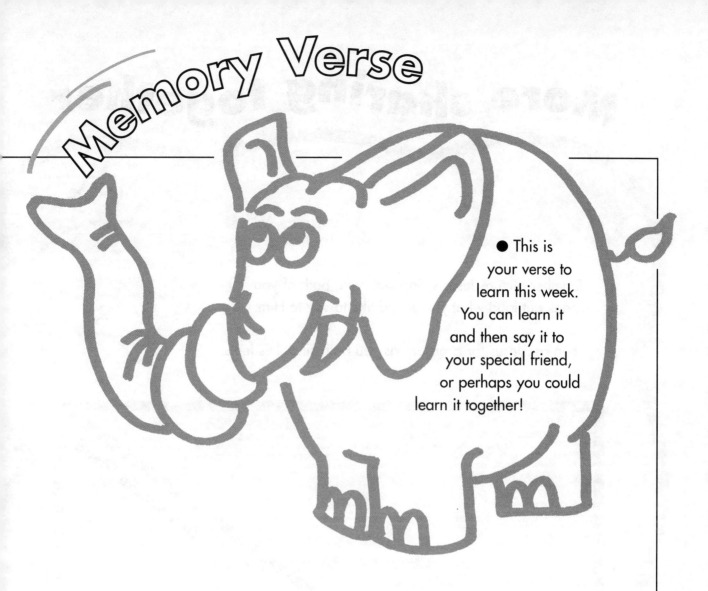

● This is your verse to learn this week. You can learn it and then say it to your special friend, or perhaps you could learn it together!

God has given us eternal life,
and this life is in
His Son.

1 John 5:11

More sharing together

Together picture Jesus sitting with you. Both of you speak out loud what you would like to say to Him.

Then ask Jesus for a picture as you both sit at His feet.

Your special friend

You

Tell each other what you think your pictures tell you.

Remember, always show your pictures and words from Jesus to your special friend, or your church leader, so they can check that they agree with the _ _ _ _ _.

If you have any questions from this unit, write them here to ask your special friend.

_____

_____

_____

_____

_____

_____

_____

_____

135

Unit 4
Love for me and love for others

Love for me and love for others

ove for me and
love for others

Jesus was in Heaven with His Father. He had always been with Him, surrounded by everything that was wonderful.

Draw a small picture, or symbol, by each of these words that tells us what Jesus was surrounded with in Heaven. You could both draw some.

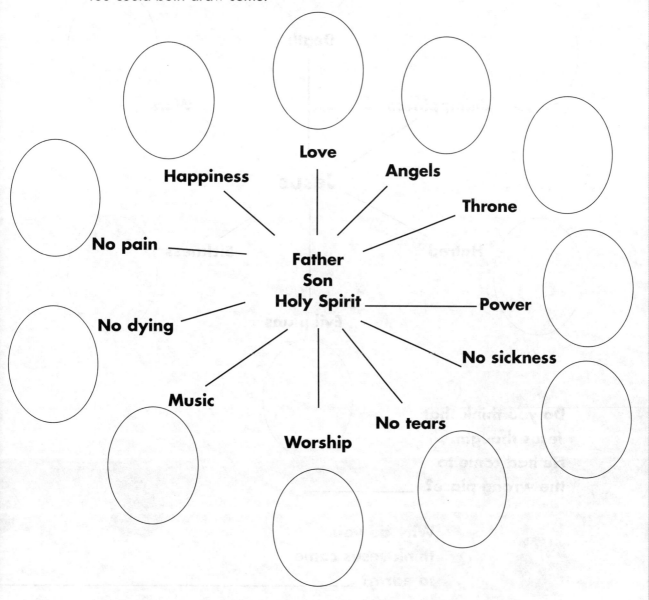

Love

Happiness

Angels

Throne

No pain

**Father
Son
Holy Spirit**

Power

No dying

No sickness

Music

No tears

Worship

Heaven is more wonderful than we can ever imagine.

**Then God sent His Son, His only Son to earth,
and Jesus agreed to come.**

Jesus was now surrounded by sin.

Now draw a small picture or symbol that tells us what Jesus was surrounded by
on earth. You could both draw some.

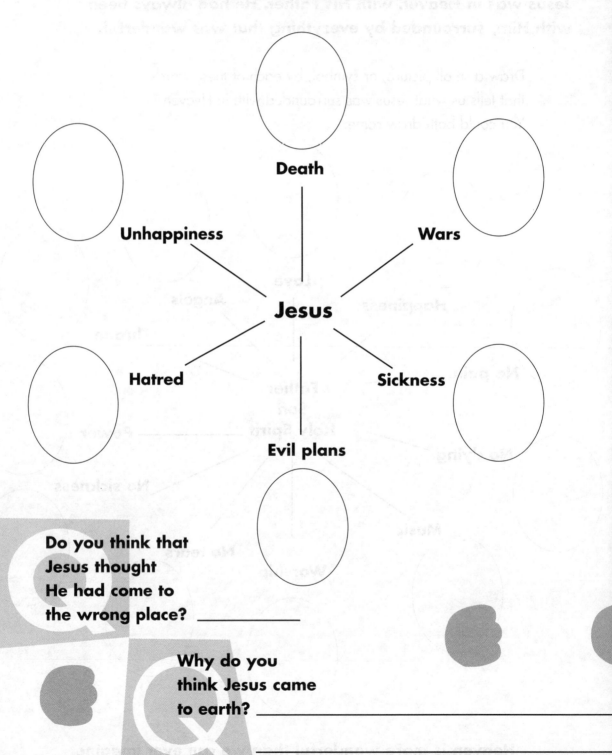

Death

Unhappiness　　　　　　　　**Wars**

Jesus

Hatred　　　　　　　　**Sickness**

Evil plans

**Do you think that
Jesus thought
He had come to
the wrong place?** _____

**Why do you
think Jesus came
to earth?** _____

_____

He came because His love was **so great** that He wanted to bring the Kingdom of God to

EVERYONE

Circle the people God did **not** want to bring the Kingdom of God to:

Good people   **Liars**

Bullies   **Murderers**   **Cheats**

Thieves   **Angry people**

I hope you did not circle any of them.

Jesus came because

EVERYONE

was loved by Him

That's why he lived on earth – among us – in a body like ours.

Read John 3:16

_ _ _ so _ _ _ _ _ the _ _ _ _ _ that he _ _ _ _

His one and only _ _ _ .

Memory Verse

● This is your verse to learn this week. You can learn it and then say it to your special friend, or perhaps you could learn it together!

Everyone

who believes

in Him

may have eternal life.

John 3:15

More sharing together

1. Both of you make a list of three people you know who don't know Jesus yet.

_____   _____

_____   _____

_____   _____

 2. Talk to your special friend about one of them.

Now pray for that person.

3. Ask your special friend to talk to you about one person they wrote down.

Now pray for that person.

The enemy

The enemy

When one sports team plays against another,
they learn about each other's tricks and plans,
so they can BEAT the opposition and WIN.

Satan is our **enemy.**

He is a **liar** who never tells the truth.

He is full of **dirty tricks.**

Satan likes to have everyone in his prison

and tries to make sure their **minds** are full of darkness,
so they cannot see the **LIGHT** of the world.

JESUS

We were once in

but now we are

Read 1 John 5:19

(it is near the back of the Bible).

'We know that we are children of _ _ _ and that the whole _ _ _ _ _ is under the control of the _ _ _ _ _ _ _.'

How can we help people who are in Satan's darkness?

We need to **PRAY and PRAY** and not give up; and to **LOVE**, because Satan cannot win against these weapons.

Memory Verse

● This is your verse to learn this week. You can learn it and then say it to your special friend, or perhaps you could learn it together!

Behold,

I am coming soon!

Revelation 22:12

More sharing together

1. Remember that we have to pray, pray, pray and not give up.

2. So pray together again for the people you prayed for last week.

3. Now make some plans about how you can show one of them this week that you really care about them.

Pray together about these plans.

Standing in
the gap

Standing in the gap

Julie was in trouble and she needed **the teacher** to help her. **She** did not know how to ask **the teacher** or where **the teacher** was, so her friend **Ann** went to **the teacher** and led **Julie** to **the teacher** so **the teacher** could help her.

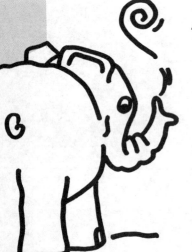

Ann '**stood in the gap**' and helped Julie go to her teacher.

I am going to write that story again and leave spaces.
In every space I want you to write either
'Jesus' instead of 'teacher', or your name instead of 'Ann'.

Then see how the story changes!

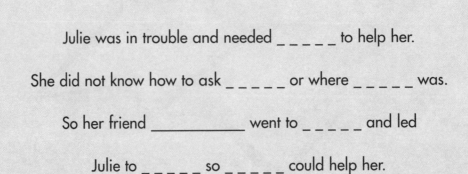

Julie was in trouble and needed _ _ _ _ _ to help her.

She did not know how to ask _ _ _ _ _ or where _ _ _ _ _ was.

So her friend _ _ _ _ _ _ _ _ _ went to _ _ _ _ _ and led

Julie to _ _ _ _ _ so _ _ _ _ _ could help her.

(Fill in the missing words.)

God was looking for someone

who would stand before him

'in the _ _ _ on behalf of the _ _ _ _ '

and there wasn't anyone.

> I think it is very sad
> that God could
> find no one.

Go back and read the second story where you put your name.

In that story, who helps Julie find Jesus?

_____

So who stood 'in the gap' for her?

_____

(You did!)

If you are willing to pray for others and 'stand in the gap'

for them, put your name here.

_____

will 'stand in the gap' and pray for others.

Memory Verse

● This is your verse to learn this week. You can learn it and then say it to your special friend, or perhaps you could learn it together!

As I have loved you,
so you must love
one another.

John 13:34

More sharing together

God is looking for people to 'stand in the gap' for their friends.

Which people do you both know who aren't in the Kingdom of God, who you could 'stand in the gap' for? Put their names on the top line (one person each).

Pray Love Pray	Put your name here	Pray Love Pray

JESUS

Write a prayer here for them:

_____

_____

_____

_____

_____

_____

_____

_____

Pray Love Pray	Put your name here	Pray Love Pray

JESUS

Write a prayer here for them:

_____

_____

_____

_____

_____

_____

_____

_____

Love without limits

Love without limits

What would you like to be when you leave school? _____

How much money would you like to have? _____

What new toy would you like to buy? _____

What would you like to be really good at? _____

If you had all these things, would Jesus LOVE you any more than He does now?   **Yes/No**

Satan lies, to trick us into thinking that we are loved
because of what we DO or HAVE.

Jesus loves us just as we are.
He loves who we are.

If you went out to play and two children came along –

**Jo had a new bike and smart clothes,
Jane wore torn clothes and was smelly –**

who would you want to play with?

_____

Who would you love most – Jo or Jane? _____

Who would Jesus love most – Jo or Jane? _____

Jesus loves them both the same – and that is the love He wants us to have for

EVERYONE

Now read James 2:1-4 and draw a picture
of what is happening in those verses.

Then read verse 8 and draw a picture for that verse.

Memory Verse

● This is your verse to learn this week. You can learn it and then say it to your special friend, or perhaps you could learn it together!

I looked for a man
who would build up
the wall and stand before me
in the gap
on behalf of the land.

Ezekiel 22:30

More sharing together

 1. Ask your special friend what they wanted to be when they grew up.

2. Ask them to tell you what job they do now and how they spend their time during the day.

3. Pray for your special friend in the work they do.

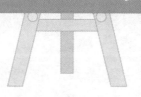

4. Now tell your friend what you do at school. Tell them what you enjoy and what you find difficult.

5. Now ask your friend to pray for you.

Agape love

Agape love

Write a list of the people you love.

_____

_____

_____

_____

_____

_____

Now put a tick next to their name if you like them.
I expect you like all the people you love.

**Jesus asks us to love people we don't find easy to love.
Can you think of anyone whose behaviour you really don't like?**

_____

How are you really going to love them? _____

Jesus loved us enough to die for us,
even when we behaved badly.
He had a special love – it was called

AGAPE

(That's a Greek word.
It sounds like this:
a-ga-pay.)

'While we were still _ _ _ _ _ _ _ Christ
_ _ _ _ for _ _ .'

Let's pretend . . .

You are coming home from school and a child
your age calls you horrible names, then pushes you over.
Your arm is broken and you have to go to hospital.

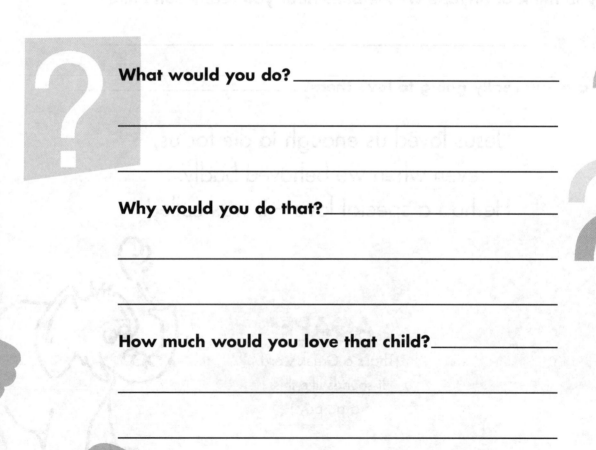

A few days later you are going to the shops and
you see the same child crying.

What would you do?_____

_____

_____

Why would you do that?_____

_____

_____

How much would you love that child?_____

_____

_____

The love we have is not enough.

We need Jesus' love.

We need *agape* love (Jesus' love).

Agape love would comfort and help that child who had hurt you.

You can ask Jesus to give you *agape* love for the person you find hard to love.

You will need the gifts the Holy Spirit gives you.

Here are some of the gifts . . .

All wrapped up in love

saying the right thing

helping others who are upset

showing others what to do when they don't know

praying for others to be healed

AGAPE

Memory Verse

● This is your verse to learn this week. You can learn it and then say it to your special friend, or perhaps you could learn it together!

Keep the royal law
found in Scripture,
'Love your neighbour
as yourself'.

James 2:8

170

More sharing together

1. Ask your special friend to tell you about a time when they were at school and they really had trouble loving someone.

2. Both of you pray for that person now – even if you don't know where they are today.

3. Now pray together for the person whose behaviour you don't like (see page 167)

4. Then both pray for you to be filled with *agape* love for them.

Building
them up

Building them up

Have you ever felt really sad or lonely? _____

When you feel sad or lonely is there someone who helps you to feel happy again?

_____

Everyone feels unhappy sometimes.

sad

happy

Everyone needs people who will make them feel happy again.

When you are in trouble and you feel knocked
down inside, you need a friend.
When your friend, or someone else you know,
is in trouble and they feel knocked down inside,

they need you to help build them up again.

Read Romans 15:2

'Each of us should p _ _ _ _ _ his neighbour for his good,

to _ _ _ _ _ him _ _ .'

How can you do that?
We have talked about many ways the Holy Spirit will help us to

build up and serve others

Q **Can you remember some of the gifts the Holy Spirit gives us?**

How many of the good gifts can you find in this apple?
(See page 72 or read Galatians 5:22, 23.)

```
P F R U I T Y H R F G M G
U Z I P Q S T B C A G M G
N P T S E F C R W I X Z O
F E T I J I H P X T U V O
N U S L L T O A N H K U D
E S E J O Y U T A F O H N
I S L F V G Y I L U J S E
P O F P E A C E G L O T S
R S C P E K I N D N E S S
L E O S S C E C W E N T C
G E N T L E N E S S S H R
A N T Y H D V I A S L O W
T U R O T P A I A A K O Y
E P O A C N A N H O R D Y
F I L T A S W R O U P A L
```

Everything wrapped up in Jesus' a _ _ _ _ love.

175

Memory Verse

● This is your verse to learn this week. You can learn it and then say it to your special friend, or perhaps you could learn it together!

While we were still sinners, Christ died for us.

Romans 5:8

More sharing together

1. How can you both help other people when they feel unhappy?

2. Ask your special friend to tell you about a time when they helped someone who was not happy.

3. Tell your friend about a time when you helped someone who was not happy.

4. Think about people in your church.

   Is there someone who needs cheering up? Make plans to do something together this week for them.

   Pray together about those plans.

Running
the race

Running the race

**Have you ever
run in a race?**   Yes/No

Have you ever won?   Yes/No

**Would you like to run in a race
where everyone can be a winner?   Yes/No**

I've got

GOOD NEWS
for
YOU

You are in a race where everyone can be a winner and

Jesus will give out the prizes!

We are children and servants of the King of kings,
living in the Kingdom of God among people who don't know Jesus.

This is the race:

Life in the Kingdom of God

Start. GO!   **Finish
                                                                   with Jesus.**

**Children and servants of the King of kings – bringing
others into the Kingdom.**

When you run in a race, you only think about things
that will help you to run well – and that is the same
for the race that we are in.

Read Acts 20:24

'If only I may f _ n _ _ _ the r _ _ _
and complete the task the
L _ _ _ Jesus has given m _ .'

I pray

**'Lord, let my heart be ready for
whatever you give me to do.'**

Would you like to pray that too? _____

181

● This is your verse to learn this week. You can learn it and then say it to your special friend, or perhaps you could learn it together!

If only I may finish the race
and complete the task
the Lord Jesus
has given me.

Acts 20:24

More sharing together

1. Talk about what happened when you reached out to the person who needed cheering up.

Pray for them.

2. Ask your special friend which sports they like and if they have ever won any competitions.

3. Now share together what you both think it will be like when Jesus gives you the prize in heaven.

Looking back
and going on

Looking back and going on

When we were talking about *agape* love (pages 167-171), why did we say it was special? _____

_____

You told me about someone whose behaviour you really didn't like. Who was it?

_____

How are you getting on with your love *(agape)* for them? Tick the box that tells me how you are feeling.

- [ ] I still can't feel love *(agape)* for them.
- [ ] It is getting easier.
- [ ] It is fine now. I really feel love *(agape)* for them.

I would like you to spend some time talking to Jesus about them

Dear Lord Jesus,

                                                        Amen.

Now I'd like you to listen to Jesus and see what He wants to say to you about them.

Lord Jesus, please will you speak to me about

_____ (put their name here)

I spent some time listening to Jesus. I asked Him about **you**.

Lord Jesus, please speak to me about all the children who will read this.

This is what He said:
I want them all to know how very special they are to me and how very much I love them.
I enjoy the time they spend with me. I am always ready to listen and speak to them.
I am never too busy.

Once I opened my arms wide and died for them. Today I open my arms wide so they can run to me and be held safely and lovingly.

I will never, ever leave them.

Jesus.

Memory Verse

● This is your verse to learn this week. You can learn it and then say it to your special friend, or perhaps you could learn it together!

Love is patient, love is kind.

1 Corinthians 13:4

More sharing together

1. Both of you get a piece of paper.

2. Now I want your special friend to write a letter to you, telling you all the special things they see in you.

3. At the same time I want you to write a letter to, or draw a picture of, your special friend, telling them all the special things you see in them.

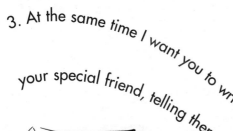

4. You read to your special friend the letter you have written about them and then give it to them. Now let your special friend read the letter they have written to you, and then you can keep it.

5. Now pray for each other.

189

If you have any questions from this unit, write them here to ask your special friend.

_____

_____

_____

_____

_____

_____

_____

z
z
z

Unit 5
Strongholds

195

The soul

The soul

Today I want to talk to you about a part of you called the

SOUL

Have you ever heard anyone talking about the soul? Yes/No

I'll explain it to you, then you will understand when you hear it again.

Your body has different parts –
hands, legs, ears, arms, feet.

> Your **soul** has different parts . . .
>
> your **mind** – where you do your thinking;
>
> your **will** – where you choose;
>
> your **emotions** – where you feel things like
> happiness, sadness,
> excitement, fear.

So

I **think** in my

mind

I **choose** with my
will

I **feel** with my

emotions

198

Q Can you fill in the spaces?

My soul

My
_ _ _ _
is where I
THINK

My
_ _ _ _ _ _ _ _
are where I
FEEL

My
_ _ _ _
is where I
CHOOSE

If you put them all together it makes your **SOUL.**

My MIND
is where I

_ _ _ _ _ _

My WILL
is where I

_ _ _ _ _ _

**THIS IS
MY SOUL**

My EMOTIONS
are where I

_ _ _ _

So –

I THINK about Jesus in my _____ I **FEEL** His joy in my _____

I CHOOSE to follow Him in my _____ Then my **SOUL** is praising Jesus.

Praise the Lord,
O my _ _ _ _

THINK about Jesus

CHOOSE to follow Him

and **FEEL** Him with you.

Then you can say, like Mary in Luke 1:46

'**My soul** _ _ _ _ _ _ _ _ (that means *praises*) **the Lord.**'

My

S O U L

PRAISES THE LORD

You could colour this.

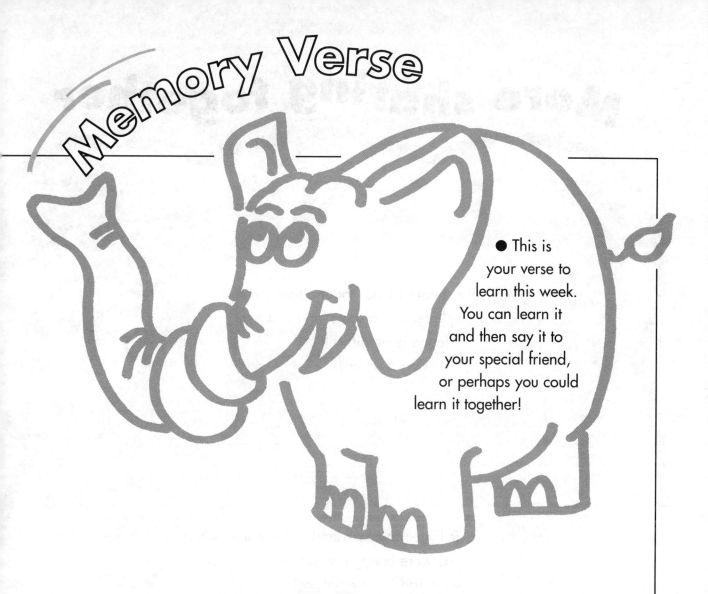

Memory Verse

● This is your verse to learn this week. You can learn it and then say it to your special friend, or perhaps you could learn it together!

Praise the Lord,
O my soul.
I will praise the Lord
all my life.
I will sing praise to my God
as long as I live.

Psalm 146:1, 2

More sharing together

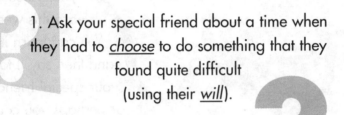

1. Ask your special friend about a time when they had to _choose_ to do something that they found quite difficult (using their _will_).

2. Tell your special friend about a time when you were happy and a time when you were sad (your _emotions_).

3. Share with each other something you _think_ about very often (your _minds_).

Having a
stronghold

Having a stronghold

In the kingdom controlled by Satan sin doesn't matter. You can walk about and not worry about sins.

Satan's kingdom

Stealing

Cheating

Bad friendships

Watching horrible TV programmes

Using money wrongly

When the Kingdom of God begins to invade Satan's kingdom, there is a

WAR

These things try to stop the Kingdom of God – they put up a fight.

They become **STRONGHOLDS.**

They **HOLD ON STRONGLY**

TO SATAN'S LAND.

THEY HOLD ON SO STRONGLY

that nothing you do seems to be able to get them out of your life.

BUT

is there anything that has such a stronghold that it can beat

Jesus?

NO!

2 Corinthians 10:4
says that we have weapons and that the weapons we fight
with are not like the ones we have in the world, but they have

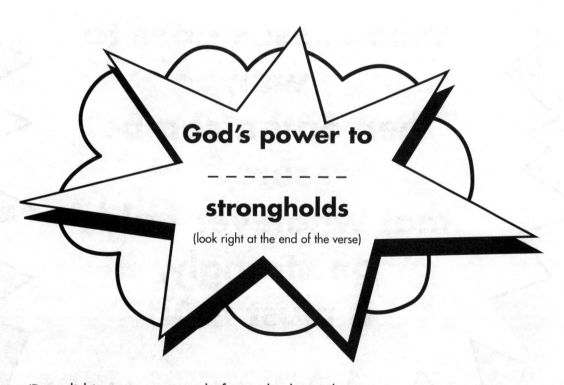

God's power to

_ _ _ _ _ _ _

strongholds

(look right at the end of the verse)

'Demolish' means to get rid of completely, so there is
nothing left at all. That is what can happen to a
stronghold when God's power is released against it!

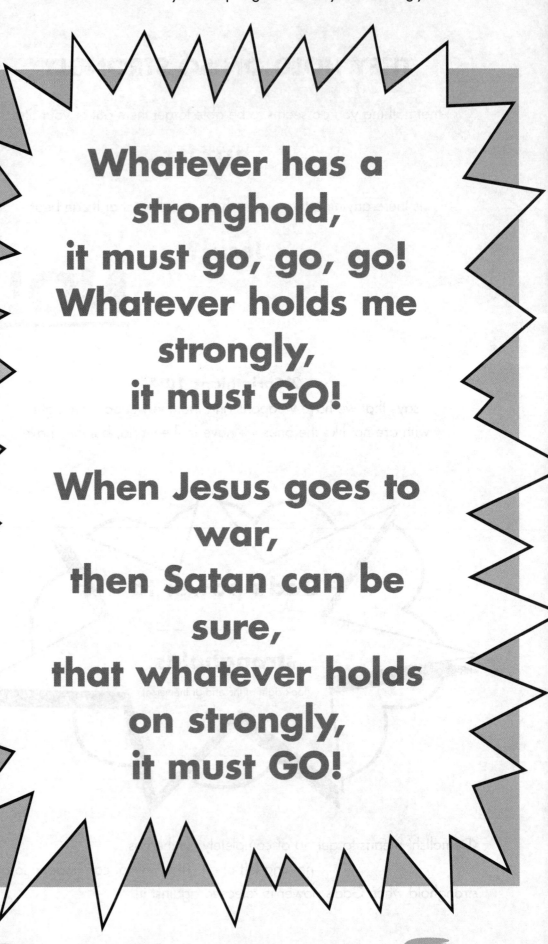

Whatever has a
stronghold,
it must go, go, go!
Whatever holds me
strongly,
it must GO!

When Jesus goes to
war,
then Satan can be
sure,
that whatever holds
on strongly,
it must GO!

Memory Verse

● This is your verse to learn this week. You can learn it and then say it to your special friend, or perhaps you could learn it together!

The weapons we fight with
are not the weapons
of the world . . .
they have divine power
to demolish strongholds.

2 Corinthians 10:4

More sharing together

First – get some small

boxes. Write different

strongholds on them together.

Then – build a tower, say the rap on page 206 together and demolish the tower completely.

Pray to Jesus, thanking Him that He can demolish the strongholds in your lives.

Rejoicing souls

Rejoicing souls

We have talked about your soul and about strongholds. Let's see what happens when we put these two things together.
But first read back over the pages you have already been through.

Have you read them?   **Yes/No**

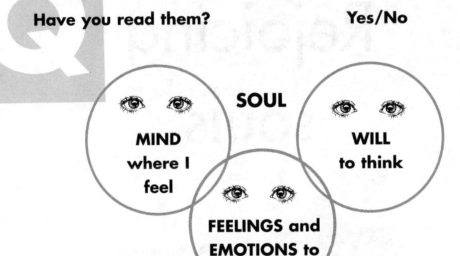

Can you find the mistakes in these drawings?
Put a circle round every mistake you can find.

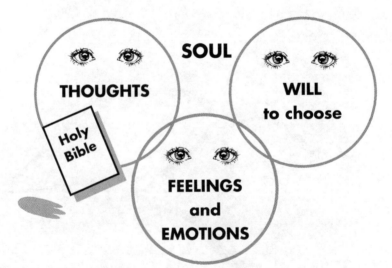

You can colour th
pictures of the sou
today.
This time the soul
has pretend eyes!

In this picture, the mind has the Word of God in it. So the mind is thinking about the Word of God,
the will is choosing what to do by looking at the Word of God,
and the emotions are feeling as Jesus wants them to feel.

210

All of the soul –

the mind (thinking)
the will (choosing)
the emotions (feeling)

is looking at the Word of God and
everything is fine with the soul.

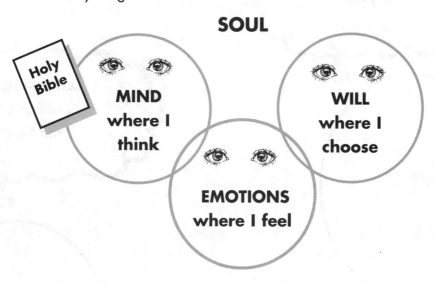

Can you think of some **good** things that
your mind could be thinking about . . .

THIS SOUL IS:

thinking –
'I know someone who is lonely'

MIND

choosing –
'I will go and visit them'

WILL

feeling –
'I am happy to go and visit them'

EMOTIONS

Could you put the faces on this soul?

212

If a child had been horrible to you, and then you saw that child crying, what would you do?

I would...

What would this soul do if it saw a child hurt and crying, **even if this child had been really horrible?** _____

That child is hurt

MIND

I will help

WILL

I am sad that they are hurt

EMOTIONS

The soul could sing **Isaiah 61:10.**
Fill in the gaps.

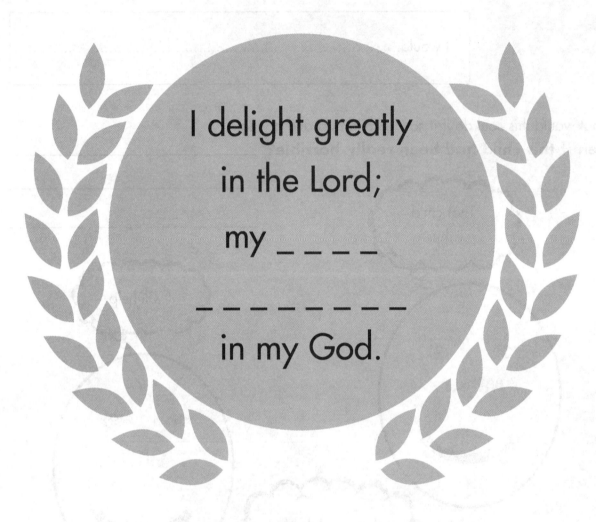

I delight greatly
in the Lord;
my _ _ _ _

_ _ _ _ _ _ _ _

in my God.

We need our minds to be 'renewed' as it says in Romans 12:2.

'Renewed' means 'made new'

If you find yourself thinking things that you know are wrong,
ask Jesus to help make your mind new.

Then you will think like Jesus.

Memory Verse

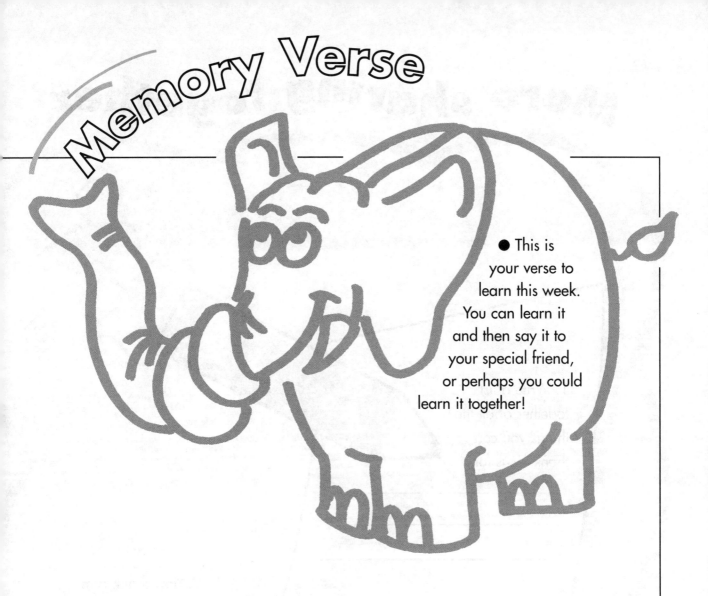

● This is your verse to learn this week. You can learn it and then say it to your special friend, or perhaps you could learn it together!

I delight greatly
in the Lord;
my soul rejoices in
my God.

Isaiah 61:10

More sharing together

1. Write a list together of all the things you can thank Jesus for.

_____

_____

_____

_____

_____

_____

_____

2. Now thank Him together for each of them.

3. Both make a 'thank you' card for Jesus, take it to your church meeting and put it in with the offering as your 'thank you' offering.

Thank you

The
enemy

The enemy

Today the enemy has entered the soul!

The enemy is from Satan's kingdom – what is the enemy?

Look back at 'Having a stronghold', page 203, and write the names of the enemy from Satan's kingdom. I have done one for you.

Using
money
wrongly

Sometimes they hold on strongly – it is so hard to stop doing these things.

They are

STRONGHOLDS

218

What happens to the
soul that has strongholds?

STEALING

Thoughts

Feelings
and
emotions

Will to choose

The soul says . . .

I want that toy

MIND

I will take it

WILL

I feel afraid of
getting caught

EMOTIONS

This person may have tried to stop
stealing but has not been able to.
The stealing has become a

stronghold.

The soul is in trouble
because **strongholds
are from Satan's
kingdom of darkness.**

219

The soul needs to cry out in the words of
Psalm 38:22

Come _ _ _ _ _ _ _ to help me,
O Lord my
S _ v _ o _ r.

SOUL

Thoughts

STEALING

Will
to choose

Feelings
and
emotions

Memory Verse

● This is your verse to learn this week. You can learn it and then say it to your special friend, or perhaps you could learn it together!

My help comes from
the Lord,
the Maker of heaven
and earth.

Psalm 121:2

More sharing together

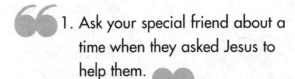 1. Ask your special friend about a time when they asked Jesus to help them. 99

2. Say the rap (page 206) together a few times.
You could use some percussion instruments, made from things in the house (check it is all right to use them first) as you say it together.

R a p

Down with strongholds

Down with strongholds!

Down with strongholds

'Come quickly to me, O Lord my Saviour.'

I need help to stop stealing. It has become a stronghold!

SOUL

Thoughts

Will to choose

STEALING

Feelings and emotions

This soul has asked for help!

Q

Who is greater, Satan who controls the stronghold, or Jesus?

Yes, but first the soul must decide that it wants the stronghold to go.

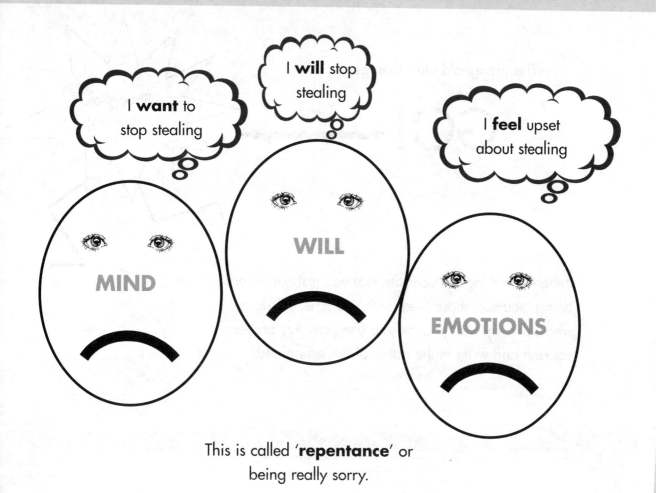

This is called '**repentance**' or
being really sorry.

Every **stronghold** is sin, and the
soul needs to repent, or be sorry, for sin.

Now **Jesus** can come with the
power of His Holy Spirit.

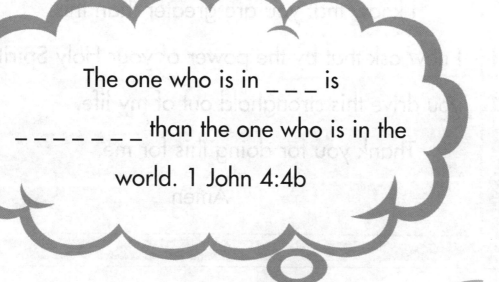

The one who is in _ _ _ is
_ _ _ _ _ _ _ than the one who is in the
world. 1 John 4:4b

The stronghold must then go

GO! ⟶

Stronghold
(stealing)

If there are things in your life that you just can't stop doing, you can share them with your special friend who will pray with you, or you can pray this prayer yourself and write in the name of the stronghold.

Lord Jesus,

I find that I keep on _____ .

I just can't stop by myself. I am really sorry that

I do this time after time and I want to stop it.

I know that you are greater than this.

I now ask that by the power of your Holy Spirit

you drive this stronghold out of my life.

Thank you for doing this for me.

Amen

Memory Verse

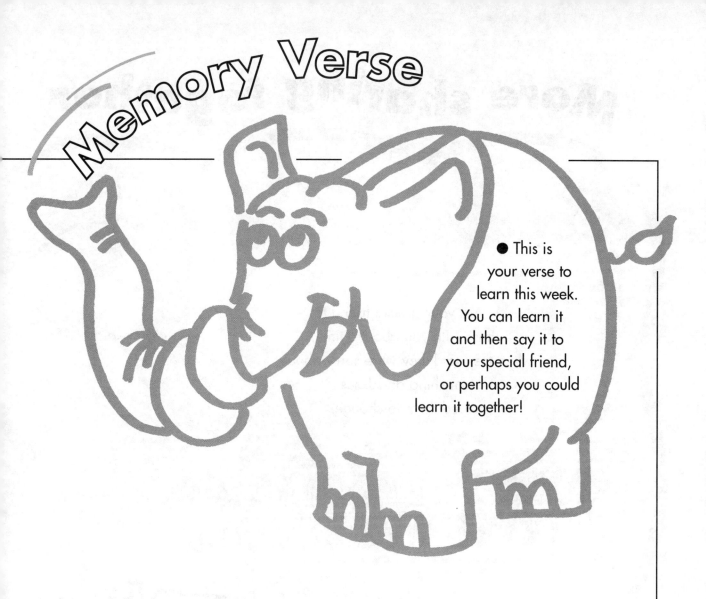

● This is your verse to learn this week. You can learn it and then say it to your special friend, or perhaps you could learn it together!

The One
who is in you
is greater than the one
who is in the world.

1 John 1:4

More sharing together

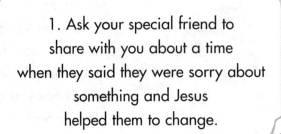

1. Ask your special friend to share with you about a time when they said they were sorry about something and Jesus helped them to change.

2. Say the rap (page 206) together again.

228

Looking back
and going on

Looking back and going on

**Do you remember talking about
the soul and strongholds?**

You prayed about something
that had a stronghold in your life.

What was it?

I would like to know how you are getting on.
Tick one of these:

☐ I still have trouble from time to time.

☐ I am free – and don't do it any more.

☐ I still have lots of trouble and need some help.

Now I am going to draw some pictures and let you put
the words in – what do you think they are saying?

Remember – every stronghold is weaker than Jesus!

Memory Verse

● This is your verse to learn this week. You can learn it and then say it to your special friend, or perhaps you could learn it together!

We take captive
every thought to make it
obedient to Christ.

2 Corinthians 10:5

More sharing together

1. Each make your own strongholds cartoon, then show them to a friend this week.

2. Ask that friend if you could teach them the rap (page 206) .

If you have any questions from this unit, write them here to ask your special friend.

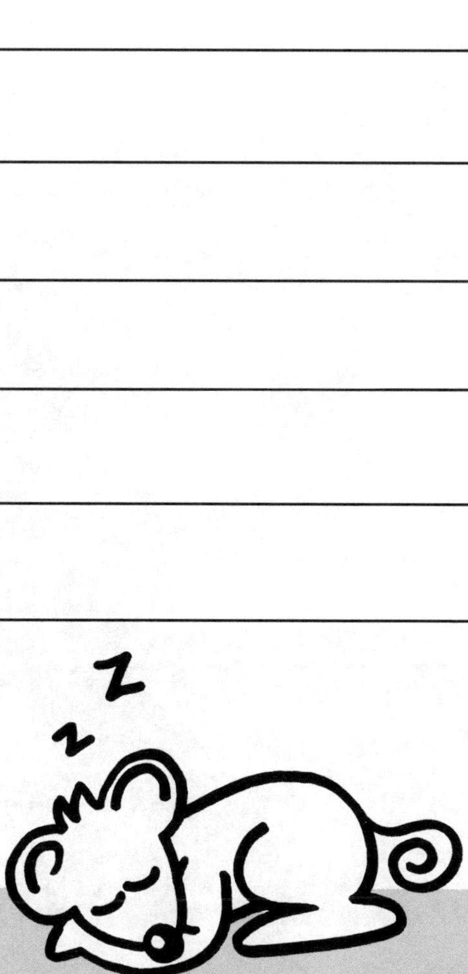

_____

_____

_____

_____

_____

_____

_____

_____

_____

Unit 6
What do we choose?

Choosing
to be happy

Choosing to be happy

Do you think that real happiness is any of these?

Tick any you think will make you REALLY happy

☐ Being happy with what I am doing

☐ Having a wonderful bedroom

☐ Being with friends

☐ Lovely food

☐ Having time to do what I want

☐ Holiday by the seaside

☐ Being the best at something

or do you think it is something else?

If you thought it was something else, what do you think brings happiness that stays deep inside us? _____

_____

Has anyone ever asked, 'Are you happy with your food?'   Yes/No

Is happiness really about clothes or food?   Yes/No

In the kingdom of the world people think that happiness is about what is around us. When the things around us change, then happiness changes too.

These are some of the things that people rely on to make them happy.

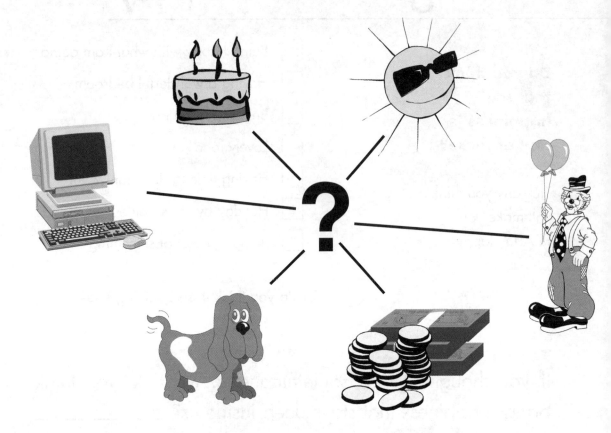

Some of these do make us happy, but the happiness does not last.

Read Psalm 126:2, 3

The people's mouths were filled with _ _ _ _ _ _ _ _
Their tongues were filled with songs of _ _ _

Something must have made them **really happy**.

Verse 3 tells us why they were so happy.

'The Lord has done

_ _ _ _   _ _ _ _ _ _

for _ _ and we are

filled with _ _ _ .'

The people were so happy because

_____

_____

We can be happy like that when we choose

to remember all the

great things

that Jesus has done for us.

In the Kingdom of God happiness is having
people we love and who love us.

Both of you draw, or write, the names of people you love –
family, friends, church members and so on.

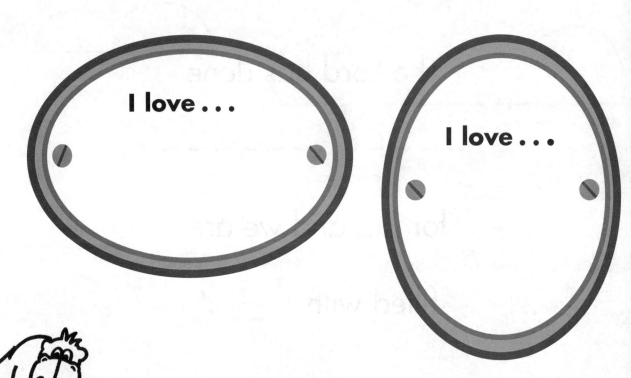

I love . . .

I love . . .

In Matthew 5, Jesus says happiness is different from having
lots of things, as we said at the beginning.

Here are some of the things He says make you happy.
Tick if you know that you are one of these people . . .

☐ Happy are the people who know they are children of God.

☐ Happy are the people who know Jesus can keep them safe.

☐ Happy are the people who know Jesus loves them.

Memory Verse

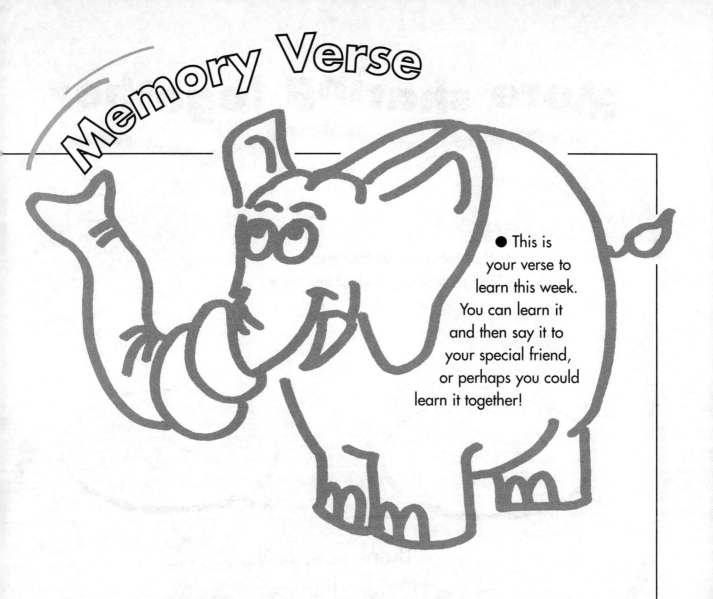

● This is your verse to learn this week. You can learn it and then say it to your special friend, or perhaps you could learn it together!

The Lord has done
great things for us
and we are filled
with joy.

Psalm 126:3

More sharing together

1. How many **great things** can both of you think of that Jesus has done for you?

Thank you, Jesus, for all these **great things** you have done for us!

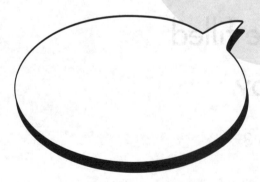

Remember to thank Him every day with laughter and songs of joy!

Happiness
and me

Happiness and me

Here are some more ways Jesus says we can find happiness, from Matthew 5.

Tick if you are one of these people . . .

☐ Happy are the people who love others.

☐ Happy are the people who bring peace to miserable people.

☐ Happy are the people who everyone knows are followers of Jesus.

There are different kinds of people.
Some people are never happy.

Some people are sometimes sad
and sometimes happy.

Some people seem to have enough happiness for everyone they meet.

Q What about you and happiness?

Jesus is interested in how you feel, so tick any
lines that tell Him about you.

People don't often see me smile.

People see me as a happy person.

**I change. I am moody. I don't know how
I am going to be from one day to the next.**

I like Psalm 150, it is a very happy Psalm.

It talks about us praising God with many instruments – making
happy music.
Draw the instruments mentioned in the Psalm;
put one in each circle.

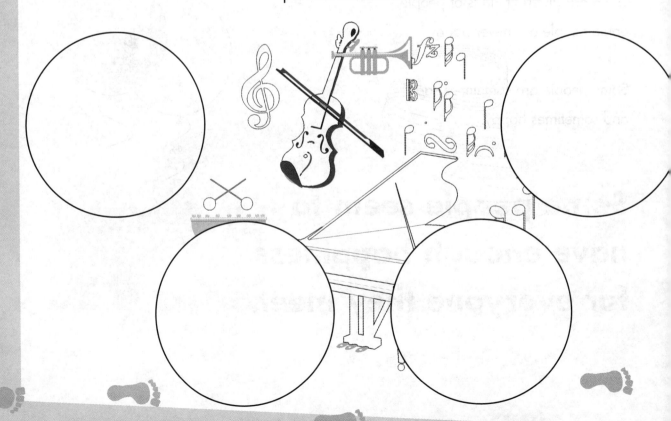

Memory Verse

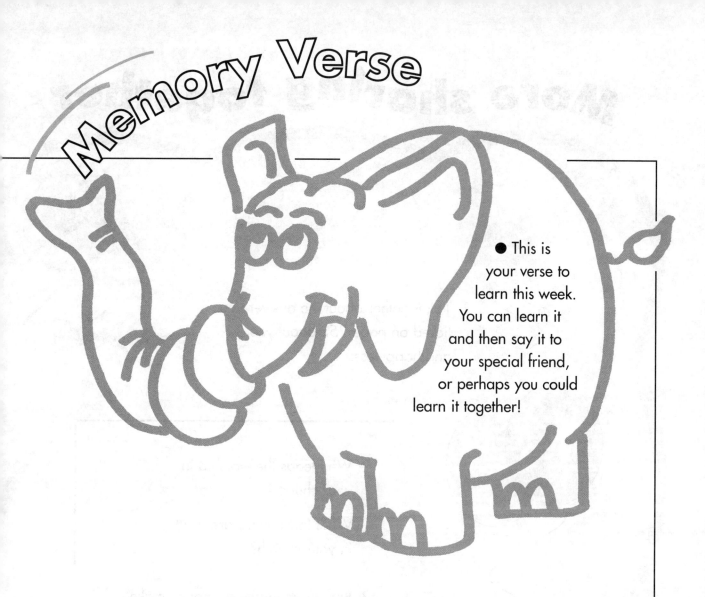

● This is your verse to learn this week. You can learn it and then say it to your special friend, or perhaps you could learn it together!

Let everything
that has breath
praise the Lord.

Psalm 150:6

More sharing together

1. Talk together about the answer you ticked on page 252 about you and happiness.

2. Who leads the worship in your church?

   What instruments are used in your church?

3. Both of you write a letter or make a special gift for the worship leader, thanking them for all they are and all they do. Arrange to go together and give it to the worship leader.

4. Pray together for your worship leader.

Choosing
to act

Choosing to act

There are some things in the Kingdom of God that are

always wrong

like lying, stealing and _____

There are some things in the Kingdom of God that are

always right

like caring for other people, listening to Jesus and _____

I am going to tell you two little stories. I want you to put an ending on each one so **THINK VERY CAREFULLY**.

John went out to the shop with Andrew. He saw some lovely sweets but did not have enough money to pay for them, so he asked Andrew to steal them while he talked to the shopkeeper. What should Andrew do?

I think Andrew should _____

_____

_____

If Andrew had done what you have just written, what might have happened?

_____

_____

_____

_____

257

Sue and Kathy were in school. Other children asked them what they thought about Jesus. Sue asked Kathy not to say anything in case they got laughed at. What should Kathy do?

I think that Kathy should _____

_____

_____

If Kathy had done what you just wrote, what do you think might have

happened? _____

_____

_____

Andrew and Kathy had to choose

Can you draw a picture, or write a story about a time that
YOU
had to choose to do right or wrong?

Andrew and Kathy had to **choose** – to upset Jesus or upset their friend.

In the Kingdom of God, when the Bible tells us clearly that some things are **RIGHT** or **WRONG** we must be careful always to put Jesus first.

He loves us very much and if He asks us to do something it is because it is best for us, even though we might not understand it at the time.

**First place
given
to
JESUS CHRIST**

Read Acts 5:29

'We must _ _ _ _ _ _ _ rather than _ _ _ .'

Peter was told not to talk about Jesus but he chose to carry on and obey God, not men.

Sometimes **we may have to choose** like he did.

Sometimes there are things that the Bible does not say a definite
'yes' or **'no'**
about – then **we need to think about other people very carefully.**

Tick which of these you do ...

☐ **I do what I want to do, even if it upsets another person.**

☐ **I do not want to upset other people but I get angry about not having my way.**

☐ **I think about other people. How they feel is really important because I feel love (*agape*) for them.**

Read Romans 14:19

and cross out the wrong words.

'Let us therefore make

some/a little/every effort

to do what leads to

upsetting people/getting

my own way/peace.'

Memory Verse

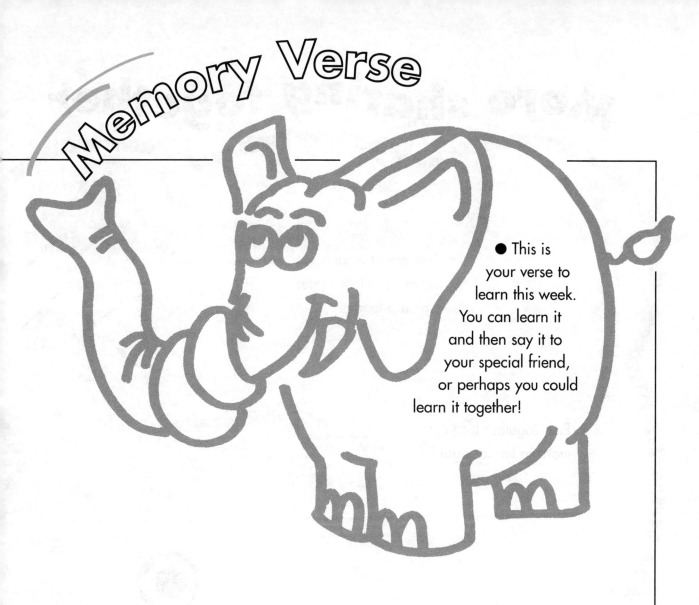

● This is your verse to learn this week. You can learn it and then say it to your special friend, or perhaps you could learn it together!

We must obey
God
rather than men.

Acts 5:29

More sharing together

1. Talk about what happened when you visited your worship leader.

2. Pray together for your worship leader again.

3. Both write a very short story or draw a picture about people choosing to do something God's way instead of their friend's way.

4. Now read the story to each other or talk about the picture.

Who's being hurt?

Who's being hurt?

Did you know that the Holy Spirit can get very, very **unhappy?**

There are some things that make Him **unhappy** and us too.

Read Ephesians 4:30

'Do not g _ _ _ _ _ the Holy Spirit.'
That means don't make Him very unhappy.

Verse 31 tells us some things that grieve Him.
Here are two – can you guess which ones they are?

A R E G   _ _ _ _

R E L A S D N   _ _ _ _ _ _ _

'Rage' means being really, really angry and feeling
you want to **destroy** someone.

'Slander' means saying words that will really **hurt**
and **destroy** someone.

Q Do you ever behave like this?   Yes/No

Circle the people who get hurt when you behave in these ways:
rage – real anger
slander – really unkind words

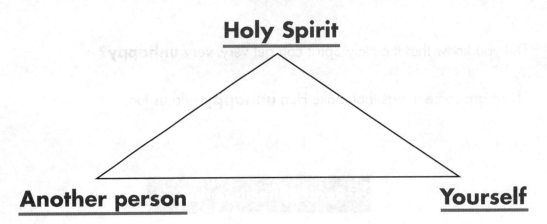

Holy Spirit

Another person   **Yourself**

Sometimes it is all these people – but the Holy Spirit is always grieved
(very hurt) and so are you.

Even if the person did something nasty, this is not the way Jesus
wants us to deal with it.

This is what Jesus did when men did something nasty to Him:

'Father, forgive them.'

**Do you think it is easy
to forgive people when
they have hurt you?**

If you do not forgive people you have horrible feelings inside you.
These are just some of them; you may be able to think of more . . .

Hate

Unkindness to that person

Anger

Wanting to get back at them

If those things are **in you**, they will hurt **you**;
so forgiving other people is for **your** sake.

Did you know that? _____

If we realise that it is best for us, too,
it makes forgiving so much easier, doesn't it? _____

The only thing that stops us is that sometimes we like having
those horrible feelings.

Oh, dear!

When you forgive, you will have good feelings inside you.
Galatians 5:22 will tell you about some more good feelings.

Kindness _____

_____

Love

Patience _____

_____

So forgiving is a wonderful thing to do!

Are there people you need to forgive? _____

Who are they? _____

Can you forgive them? _____

Read Ephesians 4:32

Here are two good ways to treat people.

N I D K _ _ _ _

G V O I G F I R N _ _ _ _ _ _ _ _ _

Ask Jesus to help you to be kind and forgiving.

Memory Verse

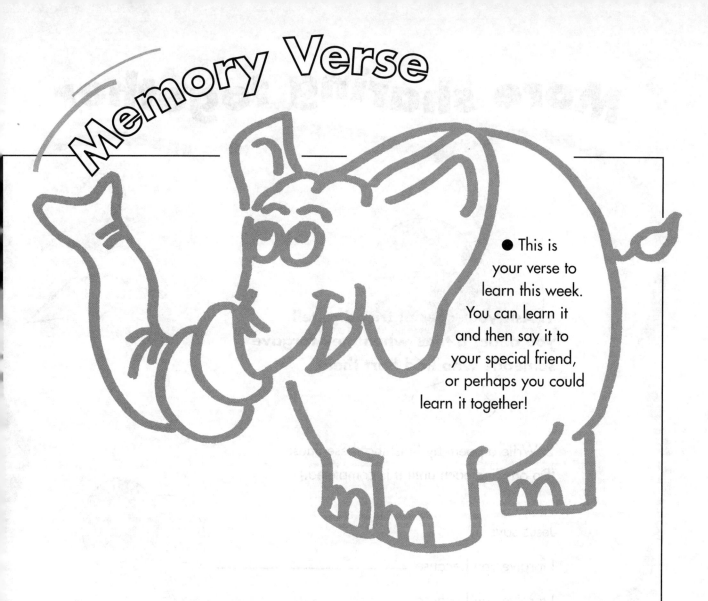

● This is your verse to learn this week. You can learn it and then say it to your special friend, or perhaps you could learn it together!

Be kind . . . forgiving

each other, just as

in Christ

God forgave you.

Ephesians 4:32

More sharing together

1. Ask your special friend to tell you about a time when they forgave someone who had hurt them.

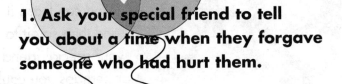

2. Write a poem by finishing these lines:
(Do one line each until it is completed.)

Jesus says . . .

I forgive you because _____

I forgive you because _____

I forgive you because _____

I forgive you because _____

I forgive you because _____

I forgive you because _____

and you never stop being precious to me.

3. Ask your church leader if you could read this together to your church group next time you share the Lord's Supper together.

Who controls you?

Who controls you?

Have you a toy or a television that has a remote control?
You can control the television – change channels,
make it louder or softer, just by pressing a button.

Read 1 John 5:19

Who controls the world?

_____

Satan (the evil one) does this in different ways.
One of these is by making us afraid of
what other people will think of us.

Read Matthew 26:69-75

Why did Peter say that he did not know Jesus? _____

_____

Have you ever felt like that?_____

_____

Peter let Satan control his thoughts and his feelings, and so he made the
wrong choice.

Look back at Unit 5, *Strongholds* (page 195). Peter let Satan control his thoughts (mind), choice (will), and feelings (emotions) so that affected his S _ _ _ .

Peter thought more of the opinion of the crowd around him than he did of Jesus. He was frightened of the crowd.

Draw a picture of this.

If you have things that you are frightened of,
Satan is able to control your mind.

Are there things you are frightened of? _____

What are those things? _____

_____

Pray together about them.

Who do you want to control your life? _____

On the next page are two names;
colour the one that you want to have control of your life.

Satan

kingdom of the world

OR

JESUS

Kingdom of God

Memory Verse

● This is your verse to learn this week. You can learn it and then say it to your special friend, or perhaps you could learn it together!

How great is the love
the Father has lavished
on us, that we should
be called the children
of God!

1 John 3:1

More sharing together

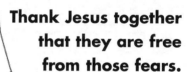

1. Ask your special friend to tell you about the things they were frightened of as a child – but are no longer frightened of.

Thank Jesus together that they are free from those fears.

2. Blow some balloons up. Both of you write things on them that you are afraid of – then take them outside and burst each balloon in turn, saying: 'Thank you, Jesus, that I can be free from . . .' (and say the thing that is written on the balloon). Then give a big clap together as the last one is burst.

If you have any questions from this unit, write them here to ask your special friend.

_____

_____

_____

_____

_____

_____

_____

_____

Unit 7
Having faith

283

What is
faith?

What is faith?

Q **What do you think faith is?**

I think **faith** is _____

_____

_____

_____

People use that word in lots of different ways.
Jesus talked a lot about **faith** so I'd like to help you understand what Jesus meant.

Write the name of one person you love very much, and who loves you very much.

_____

Now tell me some of the things that you are absolutely sure that person will do for you.

_____   _____

_____   _____

_____   _____

Are you sure they will do those things even if you are not watching them? _____

If you said 'Yes' then you have **faith** that they will do it.

means

'I'll believe it even if I can't see it'

Colour the word 'faith'.

Here are some ways of saying **'faith'** that other children thought of . . .

Knowing it will happen.

I'm sure.

Always saying 'yes' about it.

I won't listen if you say lots of reasons why it can't happen.

Can you and your special friend think of some different ways of saying 'faith'?

Read Hebrews 11:1

Now _ _ _ _ _ is being _ _ _ _ of what we hope for and _ _ _ _ _ _ _ of what we _ _ _ _ _ _ _ .

Q Sometimes it is easy to believe things.
What things do you believe?

I believe _____

_____

_____

_____

_____

Sometimes we don't believe things.
What things don't you believe?

I don't believe _____

_____

_____

_____

_____

Q It is good to believe some things and good not to believe other things –

are all the things you believe good things to believe?

_____

_____

Why do you believe them?

_____

_____

289

I am going to give you a list of statements and I want you to **tick the ones which are good to believe** and **put a cross by the ones which are bad to believe.**

☐ Jesus loves me.

☐ Church is a bad place to be.

☐ The Bible is only half true.

☐ I am a wonderful person.

☐ Jesus only loves some people.

☐ Jesus is coming back again for me.

☐ My prayers are very important.

If we have faith and believe something even though we can't see it, it is important that our faith is in things that are good and true.

Where can we find out if what we believe is good and true?

In the _ _ _ _ _

● This is your verse to learn this week. You can learn it and then say it to your special friend, or perhaps you could learn it together!

Now faith is being sure
of what we hope for
and certain of what
we do not see.

Hebrews 11:1

More sharing together

1. Ask your special friend to tell you about a time when they really believed (had faith) that something was going to happen and it did.

2. Now you share a time with them when you really believed (had faith) something was going to happen and it did.

3. Each of you think of something different that it is good to believe (have faith for).

   Pray together about those two things.

292

Faith without seeing, feeling or touching

Faith without seeing, feeling or touching

Tom and Sue were twins.
They asked their friend John
to come to their birthday party.

John was very pleased and
said that he would give each
of them a ball as a present.

Q **Do you think that John would
bring the presents as he promised?**

_____

Tom thanked John. He was excited
because he had lost his ball. He looked
forward to the party and made plans
to play football with his friends.

Sue was worried. She wondered if John
would really buy a ball. She was afraid
that he would forget, or that she would not
like it. All week she waited anxiously.

Who do you think had faith that they would receive the ball?

_____

Who was sure of something he had not seen?

_____

Tom had **faith**.

Sue was very unsure – she did not have **faith**.

Now let's think about another story.

Read Luke 1:26-31

What did the angel promise Mary? _____

When the angel told Mary that she would have a baby, could Mary **touch** the baby at that very moment? _____

Could Mary **see** the baby at that very moment? _____

Could Mary **feel** the baby at that very moment? _____

Do you think Mary believed the angel? _____

Do you think she had faith for that baby? _____

295

Now:

Read Luke 1:38

What did Mary do?

Cross out the wrong answers.

She argued with the angel.

She thought it was a joke.

She cried about it.

She believed the angel.

She had **faith** that it would happen.

Yes . . . Mary believed what God had told her
through the angel, so she had

faith

Mary was **sure** of what the angel had said and
was **certain** about the baby she had not seen.

**What was the name of the
baby that God gave her?** _ _ _ _ _

Look at Luke 1:31

There are things you can have faith for because Jesus has given us promises about them.

Read the end of Joshua 1:5

'I will be _ _ _ _ you, I will _ _ _ _ _ _ _ _ _ _ you.'

Can you see Jesus? _____

Can you touch Jesus? _____

Do you know that He is with you? _____

Will He stay with you all the time? _____

If you
said 'Yes' to the last question then you
have faith!

297

Some things that Jesus tells us are hard to believe (or have faith for).
Can you tell me about times when you find it hard to believe that Jesus
is still with you?
You can write about them, or draw a picture

Your special friend will pray with you about these.
But
this is how you can **know** He will love you and stay with
you all the time.

He said He would, and He never, never, never

_____

(put some more 'nevers' along here)

breaks His promises!

Memory Verse

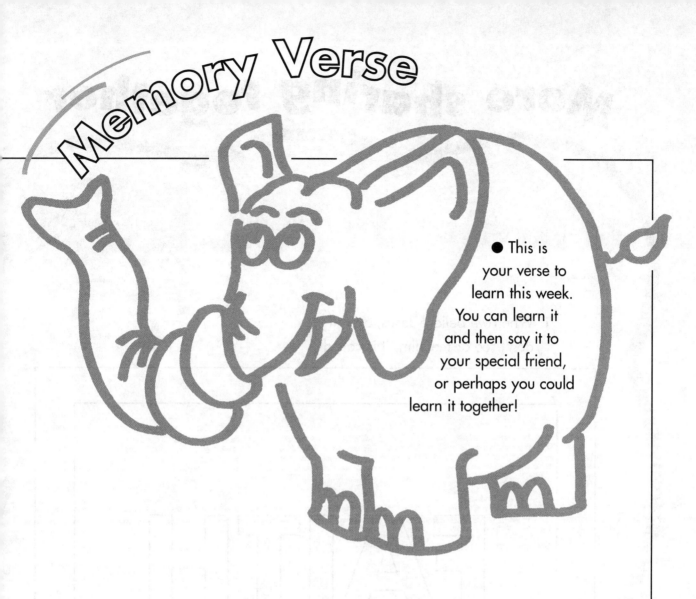

● This is your verse to learn this week. You can learn it and then say it to your special friend, or perhaps you could learn it together!

I am the Lord's servant.
. . . May it be to me
as you have said.

Luke 1:38

1. When we believe Jesus, even if we
   don't see or feel him, it is called

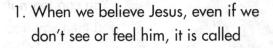

FAITH

Make your own border round the word 'Faith',
colour this in together and make this look very special.

Make a list together of things
you can't see, feel or touch but
can still believe (have faith) in.

_____

_____

_____

_____

Now thank Jesus together for them.

What about other people?

What about other people?

Read Acts 14:8-10

together and draw these pictures . . .

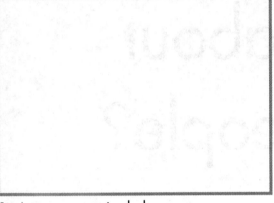

1. A man sat, crippled
   in both his feet.

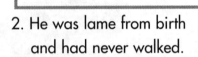

2. He was lame from birth
   and had never walked.

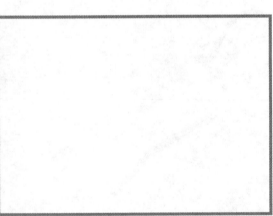

3. He listened to Paul
   as he was speaking.

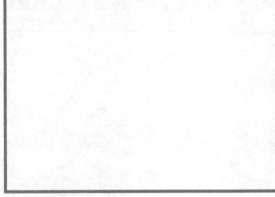

4. Paul looked at him
   and saw he had faith.

What did Paul call out?

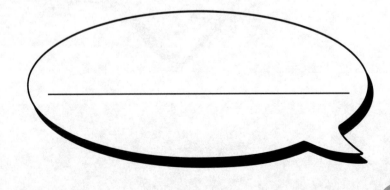

What do you think the crowd who were watching thought?

They thought _____

_____

What did the man do? Draw the picture.

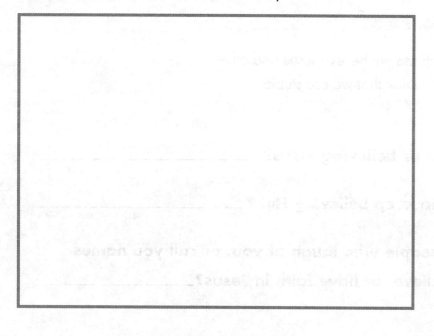

He **jumped** and he **walked**

Had he ever done that before? _____

Why did he do it this time? _____

_____

Paul . . .

spoke Jesus' words

was full of the Holy Spirit

The man . . .

heard Paul

believed (had faith)

obeyed and got up

Sometimes we believe Jesus and other people think that we are stupid.

Should that stop us believing Jesus? _____

Will it be easy to keep believing Him? _____

Are there any people who laugh at you, or call you names because you believe, or have faith in Jesus? _____

Pray with your special friend about this.

If Jesus said it in His Word, the Bible,
then you can keep believing and having
faith even if everyone laughs.
It won't be easy but
with the help of the Holy Spirit you can do it!

304

Memory Verse

● This is your verse to learn this week. You can learn it and then say it to your special friend, or perhaps you could learn it together!

Faith
without deeds
is dead.

James 2:26

More sharing together

Ask your special friend to tell you about times when they have been laughed at for believing Jesus. What did your special friend do?

Now share together about times when you have both laughed at or thought unkindly about another person.

Both of you say sorry to Jesus for those times (if you really mean it).

Pray for each other.

Believing that
I am special

Believing that I am special

Do you know that . . .

**You are God's
very special child.**

**You are born into
His family.**

You can't see this, but if you are sure of it,

and you are certain it is true – then you are His child by **faith**.

Read Hebrews 13:5b

**God has said
' _ _ _ _ _ will I
_ _ _ _ _ you.'**

Do you really believe that? _____

Can you see Him? _____

Can you touch Him? _____

How do you know He is there? _____

We know He is there because we have **faith.**

When you are frightened
Jesus is with you.

When you are happy
**Jesus is
with you.**

When you are lonely
**Jesus is
with you.**

309

**I am going to tell you
something really special . . .**

**Children have a lot
of faith and adults are
told to have
faith like children!**

Memory Verse

● This is your verse to learn this week. You can learn it and then say it to your special friend, or perhaps you could learn it together!

I will be with you;
I will never leave you.

Joshua 1:5

More sharing together

1. Ask your special friend to tell you about a time when they knew Jesus was with them, though they couldn't see Him.

   If that has happened to you, tell your special friend about it.

2. Can you think of someone who is lonely and needs to see Jesus in you, by having a special visit?

3. Arrange to go to see that person together, to show that you love them. Make a card, or a gift, together to take with you.

4. Pray about your visit together.

Keeping
your faith

Keeping your faith

Now I am going to tell you how to keep your **faith.**

Read your Bible

**Listen to people who believe
what Jesus says.**

Notice the things Jesus does for you.

**Remember to thank Him for
everything that He has done.**

**Thank Him for all the things He is
going to do for you.**

**Learn and remember some of the
things Jesus has promised.**

Let's see how you are both doing with the list that you just read.
Both of you fill in these spaces.

Read your Bible. Do you both read it regularly?

Listen to people who believe what Jesus says.
Who do you both listen to?

Notice the things Jesus does for you.
How many things can you think of that Jesus has done for you both this last week?

315

Remember to thank Him for everything that He has done.
How many times have you both thanked Jesus this week?

Thank Him for all the things He is going to do for you.
What can you both think of to thank Him for that you have
not seen yet? (That will be faith!)

Learn and remember some of the things Jesus has promised.
Can you both write down some of Jesus' promises?

Have **faith...**

What does Hebrews 11:1 say?

_____

_____

_____

_____

What do **you** say faith is now that you have finished reading about it?

_____

_____

_____

_____

Memory Verse

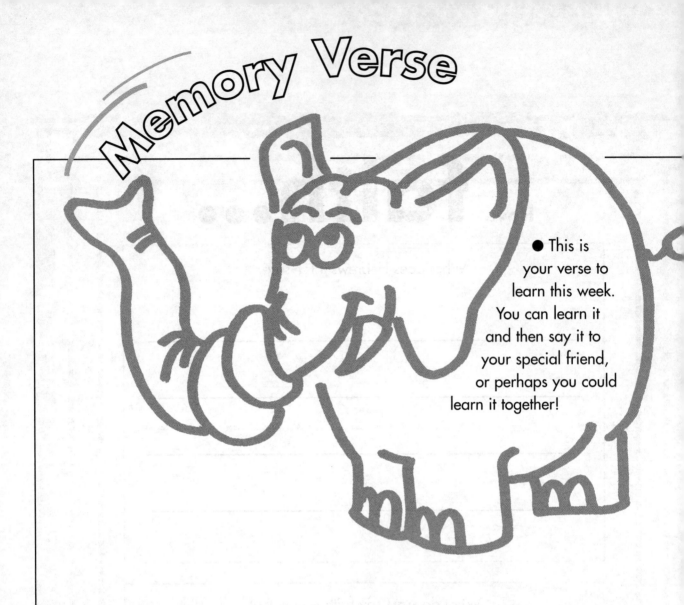

● This is your verse to learn this week. You can learn it and then say it to your special friend, or perhaps you could learn it together!

Because you have seen me
you have believed;
blessed are those who
have not seen and yet
have believed.

John 20:29

More sharing together

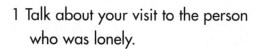

1 Talk about your visit to the person who was lonely.

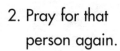

2. Pray for that person again.

3. Pray for each other that Jesus will give you more faith.

4. Now go out together into the street and pray for some of the people in the homes around you. Do this for about ten minutes. As you pray for the different homes, have faith for your prayers to make a difference.

Both of you, please write your favourite verse from this unit here

If you have any questions from this unit, write them here to ask your special friend.

_____

_____

_____

_____

_____

_____

_____

_____

Unit 8
Fighting together

Fighting together

Fighting together

I want you to look carefully at this picture.

Pretend a lion is coming – draw a circle around the animal you think he will try to catch first.

Q   **Why do you think he will catch <u>that</u> sheep?**

> He will choose the animal that is all by itself – because there are no other animals around to protect it.

Now look at this picture

These people are an army. When the enemy wants to attack, which person will be the easiest to attack? Draw a circle around him

Q   **Why do you think the enemy will choose <u>him</u> to attack?**

The enemy can attack the person who is alone, because there are no other soldiers to protect him.

328

Here is one more picture to look at.

These people are in the Kingdom of God.
Draw a circle around the person you think will be the easiest for Satan to attack.

Q **Why do you think he will attack that person?**_____

_____

_____

Satan can attack the person
who is not with the rest of
the group, because he is
not protected by the others.

Q I wonder if you are protected from Satan's attacks by having other Christians around you?

Let's have a look and see . . .

Do you go regularly to your church?   Yes/No

Do you talk to Christians, like your special friend, about . . .

   things that you are happy about?   Yes/No

   things that you are sad about?   Yes/No

Do you meet regularly with your

   special friend?   Yes/No

If you said **'Yes'** to all these questions then you are being protected, like the soldiers who attack the enemy together, and protect each other.

Hebrews 10:25 says

'Let us _ _ _ give up meeting together'

Battles are fought by armies –
and your church is a fighting squad against Satan
and his armies!

Memory Verse

● This is your verse to learn this week. You can learn it and then say it to your special friend, or perhaps you could learn it together!

Let us not give up
meeting together,
as some are in the habit
of doing, but let us
encourage one
another.

Hebrews:10:25

More sharing together

Task 1	Task 2	Task 3	Task 4
Write the names of two people in your church who come regularly.	Pray for each person by name.	Now write the names of two people who do not come regularly and so are not protected in this way.	Pray for them by name.

Both of you write a short note, or draw a picture, or make a gift for one of those people you named in Task 3.

Plan a time to go and visit them, taking your note or gift with you.

Your
armour

Your armour

We have seen this week that we are in a battle which is best fought as part of an army (your church) and not by yourself.

What else do soldiers need?
They need a **commander** who makes decisions in the battle.

Who is our commander?

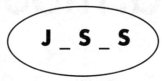
J _ S _ S

A soldier needs a book that describes what the enemy is up to and how best to fight the enemy. We have a book that tells us how to fight our enemy, Satan.

What is that book? It is the

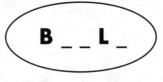
B _ _ L _

So . . .

> **You are in God's army – in the Kingdom of God.**
> **You have a commander – Jesus.**
> **You have the soldiers with you – your church.**
> **You have a book to teach you – the Bible.**

There is something else you need as a soldier:

ARMOUR!

Satan cannot get through the armour that God has given us.

In a battle soldiers often have codes to speak to each other.
I'm going to use a code – for some fun!

Can you work out what piece of armour is hidden here?

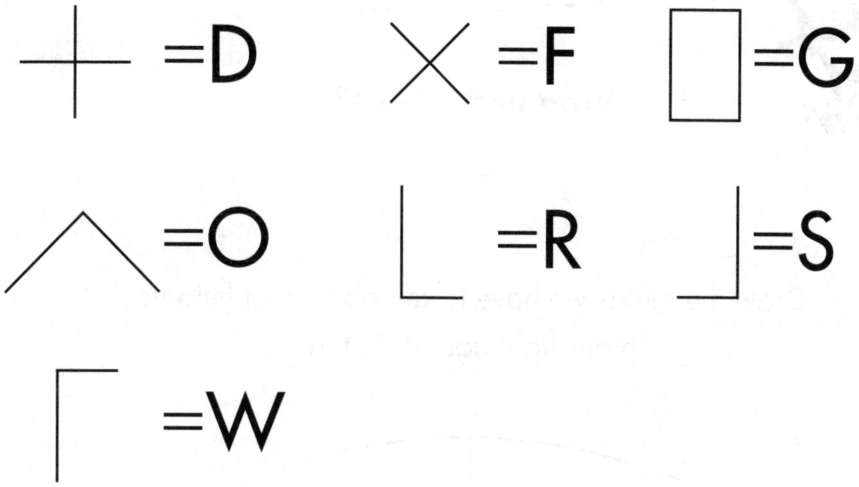

$+$ = D   ✕ = F   ▭ = G

∧ = O   ∟ = R   ⌟ = S

Γ = W

The ⌟Γ∧∟+ of the Spirit

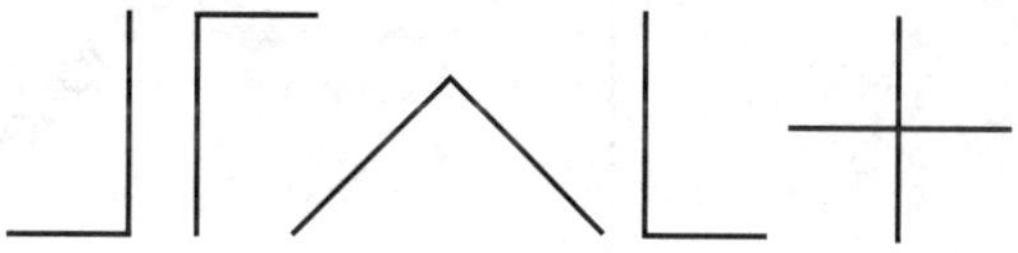

which is the

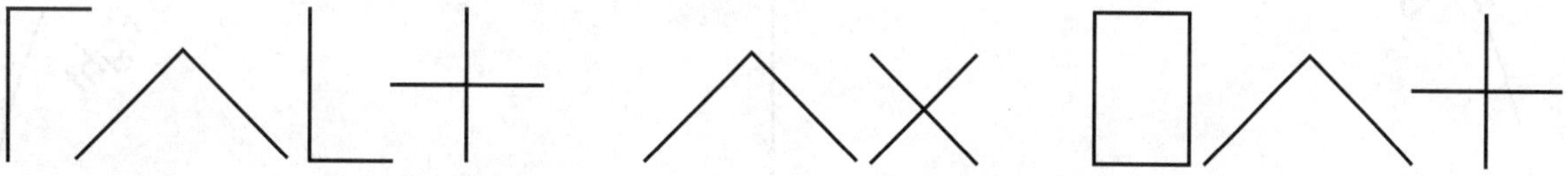

Γ∧∟+ ∧✕ ▭∧∧+

Now draw a picture of what you have discovered . . .

We have a

which is the

We can fight Satan with the Word of God! We find this in **Ephesians 6:17.**

335

**Do you ever see sheep worrying about
who will protect them?**

_____

Who protects the sheep?

The s _ _ p _ _ _ _ .

Who protects us?

J _ _ _ _ .

Draw the things we have talked about that help us
in our fight against Satan.

Being soldiers together

A book to teach us how to fight

Our commander

The armour of God

Memory Verse

● This is your verse to learn this week. You can learn it and then say it to your special friend, or perhaps you could learn it together!

Take the helmet of salvation
and the sword of the Spirit,
which is the Word of God.
And pray in the Spirit
on all occasions
with all kinds of prayers
and requests.

Ephesians 6:17-18

More sharing together

1. Talk about your visit last week.

2. Have some fun – here is a code:

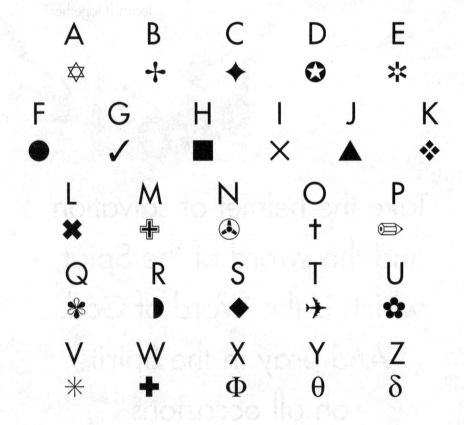

3. Write a short note to each other in code.

4. Now change papers and work out the coded message.

Rescuing
others

Rescuing others

The Kingdom of God

Satan defeated

When Jesus died He defeated Satan and made a way for everyone to come into the Kingdom of God.

That is what Satan is so mad about!
He will do everything he can to stop us winning others for Jesus.

Read Luke 10:1-2

Jesus sent His disciples out to towns and villages.

How many did He send? _____

He said that there were so many people needing

Him. They were like a harvest – and there were

only a few workers to gather them in.

Jesus needs workers to gather in the people for Him.

Who are the people you are loving and praying for, to bring them into the Kingdom of God?

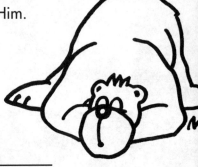

_____

Don't let Satan stop you. Here are some weapons he'll try and use.

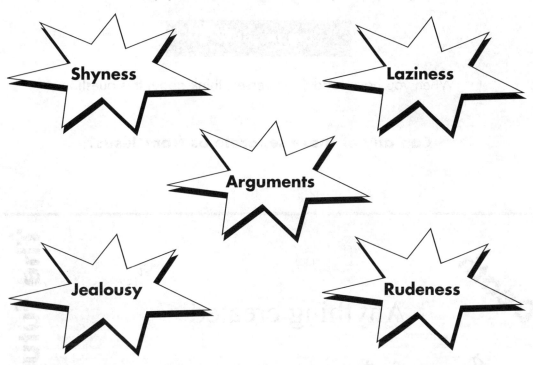

Shyness

Laziness

Arguments

Jealousy

Rudeness

Are there any others he uses to try and stop you bringing others into the Kingdom of God?

Remember to fight back!

Listen to what Jesus is saying deep
inside you – in your spirit, and use your sword,
the Word of God.

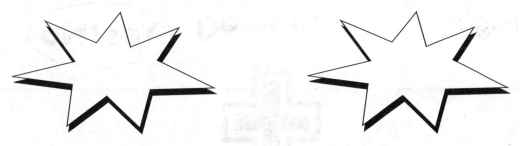

Jesus says 'Go!'

Open your Bible at

Romans 8:38-39

When you have read these verses, think about this question.

Can any of these separate us from Jesus?

Death

Life

Any power

The future

Anything created

Depth

Angels

The present

Height

Demons

Yes/No

Nothing

can separate you from the love of God in Christ Jesus.

● This is your verse to learn this week. You can learn it and then say it to your special friend, or perhaps you could learn it together!

I am convinced that neither
death nor life,
neither angels nor demons,
neither the present nor the future
. . . will be able to separate us
from the love of God.

Romans 8:38-39

More sharing together

1. Look at this map

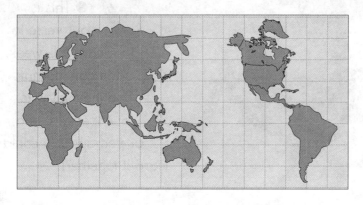

2. Choose a country each –
   perhaps one you have visited.

3. Talk about those
   countries together.

4. Both of you pray for those countries.

5. If you know someone
   in those countries you
   could both write and tell
   them you prayed for them.

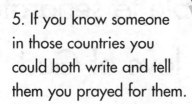

Who's in charge?

Who's in charge?

I have a play for you today. Perhaps you could read this with your special friend and two other people.

A story-teller   Satan   Jesus   Holy Spirit

Jesus (looking at some people)
Turn away from your sins, the Kingdom of Heaven is near!

Satan
Oh no! Did you hear that? Jesus is offering the people the chance to have His Kingdom on earth. I thought I was in charge here. I'll go to the desert and do something about this.

Holy Spirit
Jesus, I want you to go to the desert and meet Satan. I know that you can stand up to him.

Satan (in the desert)
Ah ha! Here comes Jesus – I'll show Him all my kingdoms and my angels who try to stop people thinking about God.
Jesus, do you see all these kingdoms?

Jesus
Yes.

Satan
If you will worship me, I'll give them to you, then you can rule them. Think how wonderful that will make you feel.
(To himself)
I don't care about my kingdoms because if Jesus worships me that will make me more important than Jesus and I'll be the winner!

Jesus

No, Satan! God says, 'Worship the Lord your God and serve only Him'. I'll never do what you ask.

Story-teller

Is there anything that could stop you putting Jesus first?
What do you want so much that you would put it before Jesus?

———————————— ❖ ❖ ❖ ❖ ❖ ❖ ❖ ————————————

I wonder what your answer was to the question at the end?

Is there anything that could stop you putting Jesus first? What do you want so much that you would put it before Jesus?

Perhaps you could think about that for a few moments.
Then write down your answer. _____
_____
_____
_____

Anything that comes between us and Jesus becomes an **idol**, and Satan can use it in many different ways.

It can stop us seeing and hearing Jesus properly, and Satan can use it as one of his weapons.

It would be like this:

God speaking

I want to tell you something really special. But you can't hear me because your money is so important to you that it gets in the way.

I think that is very sad.

We do not want Satan to win, do we?

So we need to make sure that there is nothing that separates us from Jesus.

Jesus said that there is nothing that is powerful enough to do that if we let the Holy Spirit's power deal with it.

KINGDOM OF GOD
destroying Satan's kingdoms

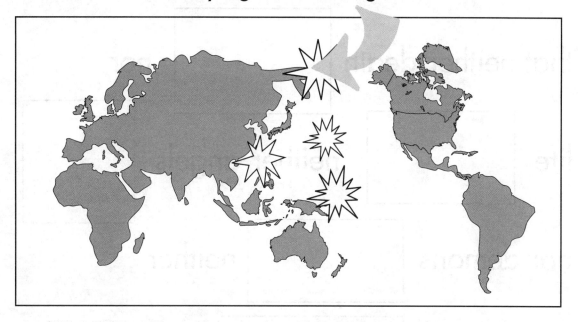

Jesus has given us armour so that Satan cannot win.
We may not be free from Satan's attacks, but we are

on the winning side

I want you to read

Romans 8:38-39

again because we **ALWAYS** need to know

how great is our God
and how powerful is
the Holy Spirit!

I will write the verse and leave a place for you
to put a picture or symbol in the boxes on the next page . . .

I am convinced (really sure)

that neither death [ ] nor

life [ ] neither angels [ ]

nor demons [ ] neither

the present [ ] nor the

future [ ] nor any

powers [ ] neither height [ ]

nor depth [ ] nor anything

else in all creation ( ) will be

able to separate us from the love of God.

Memory Verse

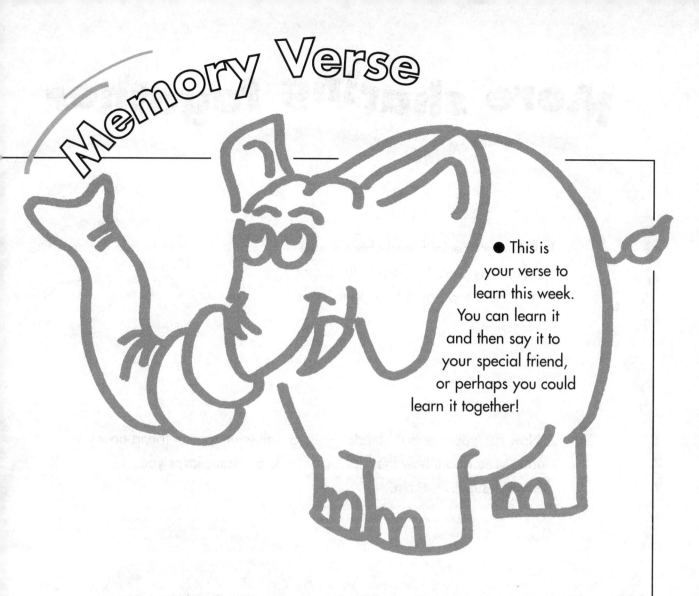

● This is your verse to learn this week. You can learn it and then say it to your special friend, or perhaps you could learn it together!

I am convinced that neither death nor life,
neither angels nor demons,
neither the present nor the future
nor any powers,
neither height nor depth,
nor anything else in all creation,
will be able to separate us
from the love of God
which is in Christ Jesus our Lord.

Romans 8:38-39

More sharing together

1. Ask your special friend about a time when they were tempted to think that they were separated from Jesus' love.

2. Now ask your special friend to tell you about how they know Jesus loves them.

3. Tell your special friend how you know Jesus loves you.

4. Thank Jesus together for His love.

5. Who has God put as head of your church?
(Pastor, Vicar, Elder)

It is good to encourage them, and show them Jesus' love.

Think of a way that you can both show them that you love and appreciate them this week.

The kingdom that will last for ever

The kingdom that
will last for ever

We saw in the last session that Jesus is the winner and living in His Kingdom makes us winners too. One day Jesus will come back to this earth and be the

King of kings

and all the kingdoms under the control of Satan will be destroyed.

WHAM!

CRASH!

ZAP!

POW!

Kingdoms under Satan's control

Read Daniel 2:44

God's Kingdom will endure (last) for _ _ _ _ .

Do you remember this?

You are in God's Kingdom
and
God's Kingdom is in you
because Jesus is in you.

Luke 17:21

So you are very special. You are in the Kingdom of the King of kings and in the Kingdom that will last for ever.

Have you ever seen pictures of people worshipping idols or gods made of stone, paper or wood?

Would you do that?   Yes/No

No, we would never worship anyone but Jesus, would we?   Yes/No

It is easy to say 'No' if we think about idols like that, but anything is an idol if it becomes more important than Jesus.

Toys – Television – Clubs – Books – Films – Computers – Sport – Games – Holidays – Money – Friends

Any of these could become an idol.

Do you think there is anything more important to you than Jesus?   Yes/No

If you said 'yes', what is it? _____

_____

Talk to your special friend about this.
Remember, nothing is more important than belonging to the

Kingdom of God that will last for ever under the rule of Jesus, King of all kings!

Satan lost the battle over death, over sin, over sickness,

over everything.

Jesus won when He died and rose from the dead.

Now you and I have a place waiting for us.

Read about it in Revelation 21:3-4,

and then both of you write down or draw
pictures of what you think heaven will be like.

Memory Verse

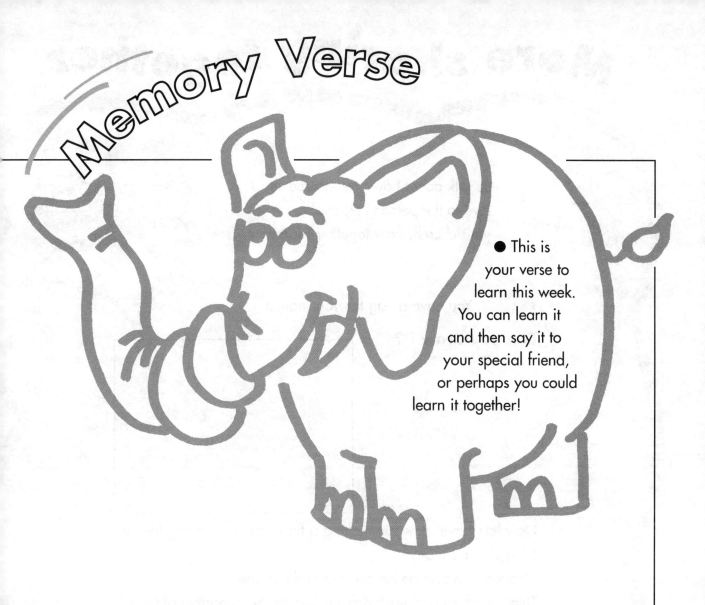

● This is your verse to learn this week. You can learn it and then say it to your special friend, or perhaps you could learn it together!

The God of heaven
will set up a kingdom
that will never
be destroyed.

Daniel 2:44

More sharing together

1. Talk about how you showed Jesus' love to the person responsible for your church. Pray together for them.

2. You have a flag for your nation.

Can you draw it?

Now let's have some fun making a flag. There is no flag for the
Kingdom of God.
I thought it would be fun for you to draw one.
Think carefully and each draw a flag for the Kingdom of God.
Think about the colours for God's Kingdom.
Think about the symbols or shapes for God's Kingdom.

Talk to each other about
the flags you have made
and why you chose the
colours and shapes you used.

So many 'thank you's'!

So many 'thank you's'!

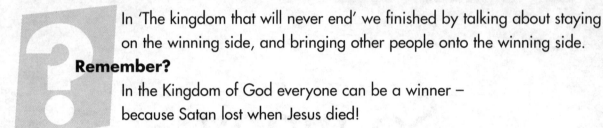

In 'The kingdom that will never end' we finished by talking about staying on the winning side, and bringing other people onto the winning side.

Remember?

In the Kingdom of God everyone can be a winner – because Satan lost when Jesus died!

We have so much to thank Jesus for. It is very good to thank Him, so both of you finish this unit with lots of 'thank you's'.

Jesus, we want to thank you for:

_____   _____

_____   _____

_____   _____

_____   _____

_____   _____

It is good to thank people too. I'd like you to write a thank-you note to your special friend who has helped you so much.
Tell them to leave the room or close their eyes while you do it.
Then read your letter to them.

Dear

_____

_____

_____

_____

_____

Write a letter each to Jesus,
thanking Him for His love.
Then listen to what He says to you.

Your letter

Dear Jesus,

Love from _____

Dear_____ , (put your name here)

Love from Jesus

Your special friend's letter

Dear Jesus,

Love from _____

Dear_____ , (put your name here)

Love from Jesus

Memory Verse

● This is your verse to learn this week. You can learn it and then say it to your special friend, or perhaps you could learn it together!

The Lord watches over all who love Him.

Psalm 145:20

If you have any questions from this unit, write them here to ask your special friend.

_____

_____

_____

_____

_____

_____

_____

_____

More sharing together

I'd like you both to think carefully about these sentences and fill them in together:

Your special friend	**You**
I think *Let's Grow!* is	I think *Let's Grow!* is
....	....
While I have been reading it my life has changed because	While I have been reading it my life has changed because
....	....
....	....
....	....
I still don't understand	I still don't understand
....	....
....	....
....	....
I know I still have to	I know I still have to
....	....
....	....
....	....

You can talk together about your answers.
Perhaps both of you would like to write to me and tell me how the book has helped you. I'd love to receive your letters.

I love you all

Daphne